# Now or Never

# Now or Never

## SAVING AMERICA FROM ECONOMIC COLLAPSE

### SENATOR JIM DeMINT

**CENTER STREET**

NEW YORK   BOSTON   NASHVILLE

Center Street
Hachette Book Group
237 Park Avenue
New York, NY 10017

www.centerstreet.com

Printed in the United States of America

RRD-C

First Edition: January 2012
10   9   8   7   6   5   4   3   2   1

Center Street is a division of Hachette Book Group, Inc.
The Center Street name and logo are trademarks of Hachette Book Group, Inc.

The Hachette Speakers Bureau provides a wide range of authors for speaking events. To find out more, go to www.hachettespeakersbureau.com or call (866) 376-6591.

The publisher is not responsible for websites (or their content) that are not owned by the publisher.

Library of Congress Cataloging-in-Publication Data

DeMint, Jim.
    Now or never : saving America from economic collapse / Jim DeMint.—1st ed.
      p. cm.
    ISBN 978-1-4555-1184-6
    1. Government spending policy—United States.   2. Debts, Public—United States.   3. Budget deficits—United States.   4. Financial crises—United States.   5. United States—Economic policy—2009-   6. United States—Economic conditions—2009-   I. Title.
    HJ7537.D46 2013
    330.973—dc23
                                    2011042590

*To Ashley, from Granddad*

# Contents

# Acknowledgments

I am thankful to live in a country where I am free to write a book that openly opposes my government's policies and where I can encourage my fellow citizens to join me in electing new political leaders who will help us save our country. And I am eternally gratefully to the men and women throughout America's history who fought and died for my freedom to participate openly in the political process.

I would like to thank my editor and collaborator, Jack Hunter, who contributed his writing skills and passion for freedom to make this book more readable and insightful. I am also thankful for all the hard work Kate Hartson, senior editor at Center Street, put into this project; and appreciative of publisher Rolf Zettersten and all the folks at Hachette who made this book a reality.

None of my work in South Carolina or across America would be possible without my staff, who inspire me every day to stay the course and continue the fight. Their remarkable commitment to the cause of freedom and their incredible talents have enabled me to accomplish far more than I could have imagined.

I would also like to thank all the citizen activists, Tea Party participants, radio talk show hosts, conservative groups, and voters who have given me hope that we can take back our country from the Washington establishment. Our successes in 2010 were, hopefully, just a foretaste of the victories we will achieve in 2012.

All my love and appreciation goes to my wife, Debbie, who keeps me grounded in the important things in life: our children, grandchildren, and friends. And thanks to all the Americans who have stopped me just to say, "Thanks for fighting, don't back down." Don't worry. As long as there are Americans who will stand with me, I won't back down. Together, we will take back our country and restore America's greatness.

# Foreword

## By Senator Rand Paul

In 2010, a historic election took place. More new members of Congress were elected than at any time in our country's history, coinciding with the formation of the largest political movement of a generation: the Tea Party.

Seven new conservatives were elected to the U.S. Senate. No single person had more influence on this election than Jim DeMint. In the midst of a banking crisis and looming debt calamity, Senator DeMint stood strong against Washington's big government solutions. When many Republicans joined with Democrats to bail out the banks, DeMint held firm. He defied Washington's longstanding tradition of "go along to get along." He continues to defy it to this day.

Time and again, Jim has stood up to the status quo politicians that the establishment continues to foist upon the electorate. For example, a significant target of voter outrage as of late has been the practice of earmarking, a long-standing Washington method of tacking on pork-barrel spending to just about any piece of legislation. After the 2010 elections, enough new leaders had been elected who wanted to change business as usual in government. By the end of the year, we finally had a major legislative victory on this important issue—and we put an end to earmarks.

Earmarking represented for many Americans everything that was wrong with the federal government, and voters threw their support behind new candidates who pledged to change the culture in Washington. Mike Lee's victory in Utah was against the party establishment that certainly had not planned on him winning. Pat Toomey's win in Pennsylvania was also unexpected. Marco Rubio had a similar win in Florida. My unpredicted victory in Kentucky represented the same dynamic.

But while DeMint's long crusade against earmarks came to fruition with the help of new conservative freshman senators, each one of us knew that it would have never happened if DeMint hadn't first waded into the emotional, internecine warfare of primary politics to endorse and promote candidates he believed would help change Washington.

Within a month after the elections, even President Obama was hearing the message. In his State of the Union speech, President Obama embraced the era of no earmarks. I joked that instead of Washington co-opting the Tea Party, we were co-opting Washington. The Tea Party was even co-opting President Obama!

But all was not won. We were, and are, winning the battle in the public arena—but we have still won very few legislative victories other than the earmark victory.

This certainly isn't from lack of trying. If the earmarks battle was a gateway to the larger issue of government spending—both in the practice of earmarking and the ensuing debate over such dubious practices—Senator DeMint has always swung that gate as wide open as possible, allowing Americans to get a real look at the damage Washington continues to work. This book surveys the wreckage and provides a blueprint for real change. Yet, for every substantive solution DeMint has ever offered, there have always been establishment spokesmen from both sides ready to immediately denounce his proposals and explain why they're impractical.

I know the feeling. One of the first things I did when I got to Washington was propose $500 billion in cuts to the budget for one year. This would have reduced our $1.5 trillion deficit by one third. My proposal would have simply rolled back federal spending to 2008 levels by initiating reductions at various levels almost across the board. I would have cut the Departments of Agriculture and Transportation, which would have saved us $42 billion each. My proposed cuts to the Departments of Energy and Housing and Urban Development would have saved another $50 billion each. I also included getting rid of the Department of Education and sending that responsibility back to the states, which would have saved another $80 billion, as well as spending reductions in international aid, the Department of Health and Human Services, the Department of Homeland Security, and other federal agencies.

Not surprisingly, liberal Democrats thought all of these cuts were too "extreme." My proposal also included cutting wasteful spending in the Department of Defense, especially considering that since 2001 our annual defense budget increased nearly 120 percent. Even subtracting the costs of the conflicts in Iraq and Afghanistan, Pentagon spending was up 67 percent. These levels of spending were unjustifiable and unsustainable—and yet too many Republicans also thought these Defense Department cuts made my proposal too "extreme."

Senator DeMint and I thought a mere $500 billion in cuts

really was a modest proposal. At one Tea Party event, the crowd told me $500 billion was a good start, but it was still only one third of one year's deficit. They were right. In Washington my proposal got the opposite reaction—blank stares and disbelief that anyone would propose seriously cutting spending. Only in Washington was the plan to cut spending considered "extreme."

This has always been the problem in Washington. Everyone can agree that we face monstrous fiscal dilemmas and yet few are willing to address them or offer real solutions. Senator DeMint rightly says that to fix these problems, it's now or never. Yet the entrenched Washington establishment still says it's not now or ever. My next proposal was a five-year budget plan that would have reduced federal spending by $4 trillion. This plan would have brought all nonmilitary discretionary spending back to 2008 levels; began the process of entitlement reform while not changing Social Security and Medicare benefits; block-granted to the states programs like Medicaid and food stamps; eliminated the Departments of Education, Energy, and Housing and Urban Development; significantly cut corporate welfare from the Departments of Agriculture and Commerce; reduced military spending; and repealed ObamaCare.

Needless to say, not one Democrat supported my five-year budget proposal. Senators Jim DeMint and Mike Lee were among only seven Republicans who supported it. Lee said that any Republican who opposed the plan had better come up with a better option. Few, if any, did.

Still, there is reason for optimism. The 2011 debt ceiling debate resulted in an agreement between President Obama and House Speaker John Boehner that gave us nothing in the way of real spending cuts, but the controversy it caused on Capitol Hill indicated that things were trending in our direction. Strong GOP support for the Cut, Cap, and Balance plan (which would cut current spending, cap future spending, and balance the federal budget) in the House signaled that more Republicans than ever were finally willing to get behind serious reform. During the debt ceiling debate, the media and liberal pundits began to wonder if the Tea Party was now in control of Washington. If only this were true.

Changing Washington's spending habits simply requires the will to do so. There are solutions on the table. I've proposed them. Senator DeMint has proposed them. Senator Lee has proposed them. So have others.

But we must keep pushing. In the following pages, Senator DeMint points the way forward, setting forth the enormity of the debt crisis on the horizon. Last year's debt ceiling debate in which so many critics said the Tea Party was now "running" Washington—well, that was only the beginning. Senator DeMint dispels the notion that conservatives have changed the culture of Washington. It should be a surprise to no one that Washington remains stubbornly resistant to change. Despite much crowing about the "extremism" of Republican freshmen, conservatives haven't changed anything yet. But we are getting started.

Senator DeMint lays out a plan for how we can take our government back. He is honest in his appraisal that we are speeding toward a cliff that resembles the bankruptcies of Europe, and that, at best, our current policies are merely slowing down our fast-approaching default. We are borrowing $40,000 per second. Entitlements and interest will consume the entire budget within a decade. The debt ceiling deal set spending caps that increase every year. My understanding of *cutting* spending is that you would spend less next year than you spent this year. Yet the debt ceiling caps still rise each year, revealing the lie that spending will be cut.

When they say the appointed Super Committee that was part of the 2011 budget deal will cut $2 trillion dollars, what they really mean is that it will cut $2 trillion from proposed increases in spending. So instead of adding $9 trillion to the debt over ten years, we will merely add $7 trillion. Suffice it to say, this is not a cut. Only in Washington can the accumulation of so much new debt be seen as fiscal responsibility.

The 2010 elections were just the beginning. Economists now argue that the looming sovereign debt crisis is the most predictable crisis in history. This crisis will be accompanied by a dramatic rise in interest rates as creditor nations lose faith in our ability to repay.

Make no mistake: The United States will not default. Great nations never default, at least in the technical sense. The checks to pay our interest will always be paid. The checks to our senior citizens will always be paid. The real question is this: Will our checks continue to have value?

Already, gas prices have doubled since President Obama took office. Food prices have risen dramatically. Gas and food prices are rising not because of scarcity but because the value of the dollar is falling.

Our debt has a face—unemployment. The Democrats want to subsidize the unemployed and we want to have fewer unemployed. Economists calculate that the debt is now contributing to the unemployment of a million Americans.

Debt is not an abstraction, not just some incomprehensible number. It is not necessary to conceive of what a trillion dollars is to understand the face of debt. To comprehend the ramifications of debt, simply go to the grocery store with a senior citizen who is completely dependent on Social Security. The rising food prices that confront senior citizens on fixed incomes are a direct consequence of our massive debt that is paid for by inflating the currency.

In the following pages, you will be both encouraged and ultimately dismayed at the problems that face our country. The debt crisis is imminent, and rather than hide and try to protect what little remains as the crisis unfolds, Senator DeMint encourages you to join the battle and not give up on the noble ideas that led to the greatest experiment in freedom ever known.

I'm not ready to give up or give in—and I hope our country will continue this great awakening, which gives me hope that America's best days lay ahead.

# Introduction:
# A Call to Action

Establishment critics say that those of us who warn about America's massive debt and impending economic collapse are alarmists. They're correct. The status quo is demonstrably unsustainable and it is unquestionably time to sound the alarm.

And this book is a call to action.

The political establishment in Washington is destroying our country, and only a determined effort by the American people can stop them. We are in serious trouble and very close to economic collapse. This is not hyperbole; Americans have never been this close to losing all the freedom, prosperity, and opportunity that generations of citizens and soldiers have fought and died to give us.

America is approximately $15 trillion dollars in debt. This figure grows every day and now exceeds the size of our total economy. No nation can survive this level of debt.

Our published, public debt obscures the real financial apocalypse that is staring our children in the face—if we keep our promises concerning Social Security, Medicare, and veterans' benefits, the federal government has approximately $100 trillion in unfunded liabilities. In the face of this crisis, Washington politicians continue to invent new ways to spend money.

This is insane.

Americans must begin to understand what caused our fiscal crisis in order to turn things around before it's too late. We are not getting the truth from the politicians or the media. This book will give you the truth and will be a handbook for the 2012 elections and beyond.

If we are to save this country it will be because enough patriotic citizens still believe America can be saved. It is in our hands. Now is the time to act.

And the next election may be our last chance.

## It's All Up to You

The United States Constitution gave us the framework to build the most successful and prosperous nation in history. It requires regular elections to ensure that our federal government remains a government of the people, by the people, and for the people. The signers of the Constitution expected citizens to keep a tight rein on elected officials. This, in turn, would also serve to limit the size and scope of the government.

Failure to live up to the Founders' expectations could prove disastrous, and their warnings to future generations are legend. Outside Independence Hall after the Constitutional Convention in 1787, a woman asked Ben Franklin, "Well, Doctor, what have we got, a republic or a monarchy? Franklin answered without hesitation, "A republic, if you can keep it."[1]

George Washington put the responsibility for maintaining our freedoms firmly on the shoulders of the people: "The preservation of the sacred fire of liberty, and the destiny of the republican model of government, are justly considered deeply, perhaps as finally, staked on the experiment entrusted to the hands of the American people."[2]

Unfortunately, too many Americans have not been vigilant. This has allowed elected officials in Washington to ignore proper constitutional limits, unleashing unintended and unprecedented government power, which now brings our nation to the brink of fiscal and economic collapse.

Our Founders knew that maintaining a free republic would require a vigilant citizenry. The responsibility for our government, our nation, and our freedoms lies in the hands of the American people. But too many Americans have taken the privilege of voting and political participation for granted. Even in the Tea Party–inspired midterm elections of 2010, only 29 percent of Americans of voting age actually voted.[3] Compare this to Iraq's first free election in 2005, when 75 percent of Iraqis voted,[4] despite threats of violence.

There has never been a time in America's history when it has been more necessary and urgent for citizens to stand up and take back our government. President Barack Obama, Congress, and the Federal Reserve are out of control, as they spend us into oblivion and print money to buy our own debt. Despite numerous warnings of impending bankruptcy and economic collapse, federal politicians and bureaucrats continue to spend more than we bring in every year. They refuse to promote sound monetary policy or balance the budget. Gross fiscal irresponsibility has become the new norm; fiscal responsibility and budget consciousness, the new extreme.

Spending and debt are not the only inexcusable excesses of our federal government. The expansion of federal control over states and the private sector has contributed to major financial problems for the states and continues to hobble the American economy. The federal government effectively controls education, health care, energy production, transportation infrastructure, communications, housing, financial institutions, and banking services. Federal agencies have expanded their control over businesses to the point where America now has one of the most unfriendly business environments in the free world. Companies are fleeing America and taking their jobs overseas. Our government that is supposed to be of, by, and for the people now regularly works against this nation's founding principles and its citizens.

Government policies with perverse incentives have weakened an American culture once renowned throughout the world for its spirit of independence, rugged individualism, strong work ethic, commitment to family, and moral dignity. For example, for decades the federal government has encouraged births out of wedlock, a major cause of poverty, school dropouts, drug use, juvenile delinquency, and incarceration. Forty percent of American children, including 70 percent of African-Americans, are now born out of wedlock.[5] Rather than encouraging independence and personal responsibility, our government continues to encourage irresponsible and destructive behavior while expanding welfare and entitlement programs that force millions of Americans into dependency on taxpayer-funded programs.

Some politicians have suggested that social issues be set aside while we address our fiscal crisis, but this view belies the real root causes of the nation's reckless spending and crushing debt. Cultural pathologies caused by the unintended consequences of naïve social policies have contributed to many of America's economic and fiscal problems. The economic crisis was caused by too much government. The same is true of many of our social crises, where the solutions must also mean getting away from government interference and largesse.

## Spending Is an Addiction

Despite the obvious threats created by the growth and intrusion of the federal government into all areas of our economy and culture, I am constantly amazed at how out of touch my colleagues are with the very real dangers we face as a nation. I cannot count the number of presentations, media interviews, and floor speeches that I and other conservative senators have given about our reckless spending and irresponsible budget deficits—yet presidents, Congress, and, for the most part, the media have summarily ignored these calls for restraint.

Why? How can public officials and journalists continue to ignore such a serious and obvious threat? I asked former Federal Reserve chairman Alan Greenspan these questions when he came by my office to discuss economic and monetary policies. "Mr. Chairman," I asked, "the people in the administration and Congress are smart people. Are they intentionally trying to collapse our economy and undermine our currency as a way to restructure our debt and redistribute wealth?"

Greenspan answered, "I don't think so. Government spending is an addiction."

I think Greenspan is right. Washington's determined drive toward national bankruptcy is more likely an addiction than a conspiracy. Attempting to persuade my colleagues to stop spending has been like confronting an alcoholic about his need to stop drinking, with the prevailing attitude being "Just one more drink and I'll quit tomorrow." The spending continues in Washington, as do the many promises to cut the budget—tomorrow. There's an old song by the 1960s rock group Creedence Clearwater Revival called "Someday Never Comes."

And it never does.

The facts concerning our spending crisis are irrefutable, but President Obama and congressional Democrats seem to wake up every morning with new ideas for more government programs and new regulations to restrict freedom. Making matters worse, there are not enough Republicans who will stand up and fight.

There is only one way to stop this madness: an intervention by the American people.

Freedom-loving Americans are in for the fight of our lives, and we are competing against determined foes who want to recast America in the mold of socialist Europe. The key to success in any competition lies not only in understanding your enemy but knowing when to go all out and put it all on the line. You must identify those make-or-break moments that may decide the final outcome of a battle. For those who've been paying even casual attention to the current crisis, it is clear that the 2012 election will be a make-or-break moment for America.

The Treasury Department has to borrow money almost weekly to pay the debts now coming due. This is like paying off one credit card with another—sooner or later, all your credit cards will be maxed out. Credit rating agencies and capital fund managers around the world are now questioning if the United States has the political will or the means to even pay the interest on our massive debt. If the federal government continues on its present course, China and other creditors will soon stop lending us the money we need to make our debt payments. When that happens, America's economy and currency will quickly collapse.

Yet despite the growing evidence that America is literally dangling over the edge of a fiscal and an economic cliff, Congress and the President refuse to even set a goal to balance the federal budget. The stakes couldn't be higher, and our response must transcend politics and partisan rhetoric. Our political system will not save us; it is destroying our country. Only a vigilant citizenry can now save America.

## We're All Americans Now

The political labels must come off—Republican, Democrat, liberal, conservative, libertarian—we're all Americans now. Hyphenated Americans—African-Americans, Hispanic-Americans, Native-Americans, Asian-Americans, and Anglo-Americans—must all stand together to promote freedom, equality, and opportunity for everyone. We must all grasp the reality that our nation and the freedoms that define it are in grave danger. Only the American people can save us from the mess created by irresponsible politicians.

It will be challenging to unify Americans around the cause of freedom because of the many government policies that have divided us. Many citizens are dependent on government programs for their income, health care, education, food, housing, and transportation. And, while over half of Americans are dependent in some way on the federal government, nearly half pay no federal income tax.[6] Dependent voters who pay little or no federal income tax are much more likely to elect candidates who promise more from government.

Government debt and higher taxes are not these voters' problem.

Those Americans who create wealth, jobs, and opportunity pay the lion's share of taxes. Ten percent of the top earners pay 70 percent of all taxes while earning only 46 percent of all taxable income, according to the Internal Revenue Service. With such a small base of taxpayers, even subtle shifts in economic activity cause major shifts in tax revenue to the federal government. Raising taxes on the "rich" results in a more unstable tax base and shifts capital from the most productive area of our economy to the most unproductive—government. Despite calls to "tax the rich," we cannot solve our debt problem by raising taxes.

Because government policies have created a divided citizenry— "givers" and "takers"—the country also remains divided over the role of government. Based on voting patterns, about half of Americans appear to believe in the centralization of power at the federal level. These voters are more likely to be government dependents and nontaxpayers. The other half supports the decentralization of power and individualism. These opposing worldviews among voters result in starkly different views about the fundamental role of the federal government, and they help explain the irreconcilable differences between Republicans and Democrats.

We must convince dependent Americans who have been misled by the false promises of government security that there is a better way. The facts are on the side of those who love freedom: we are most secure when we are most free. But rescuing Americans from government dependency and the allure of collectivism will be difficult.

We need a clear and simple message that helps our fellow citizens sift through the confusing babble produced by politicians and talking heads in the media. Developing an effective message requires an understanding of just how unique America is and how it became the greatest nation in the history of the world. Equipped with the facts, the right message, and the right messengers, we can stand together and fight.

## The 2010 Elections Proved Citizens Can Change Washington

When federal spending and debt increased dramatically after Democrats took control of Congress in 2007, and the White House in 2009, millions of Americans took to the streets in a show of unity against the unprecedented expansion of government. Citizens were irate about the Wall Street bailouts in 2008, and this anger only multiplied with Obama's takeover of the auto industry, his trillion-dollar economic stimulus debacle, his nationalization of the health-care system, and his paralyzing regulatory expansion of our financial institutions and banking system.

Thousands of Tea Party groups organized protests all over the country. Nearly a million grassroots activists came to Washington in 2009 to express their discontent at the political establishment's continued irresponsible spending, borrowing, and debt. But the politicians wouldn't listen. With large Democrat majorities in the House and Senate, Obama was able to push through much of his central planning, collectivist agenda.

I also decided to go on the offensive against the Washington establishment in 2009, which included taking on the many reckless spenders in the Republican Party. We needed to elect courageous conservatives who would join the fight against all of Washington's big spenders. The Senate Conservatives Fund (SCF) was my weapon in this fight. Our website, SenateConservatives.com, attracted thousands of small contributions from frustrated citizens in every state. We raised over $9 million for conservative Senate candidates with an average contribution of $45.

My first endorsement was Pat Toomey from Pennsylvania. He was challenging incumbent liberal Republican Arlen Specter. I was excoriated by the Senate Republican leadership for not understanding how the Senate worked. "It's not about principles," they lectured, "it's about the numbers. A conservative can't win in Pennsylvania, and if Toomey wins the primary it will cost us a seat."

The media had a field day reporting all the negative comments about me from my Republican colleagues—but I didn't back down. When asked about my supposedly naïve support of candidates who believed in conservative principles, I responded, "I'd rather have thirty Republicans who believe in the principles of freedom than sixty who believe in nothing at all." Even some conservative media commentators said I was wrong, but I knew the best way to increase the number of Republicans in the Senate was to stand for the principles we said we believed in.

The SCF endorsed Marco Rubio in Florida against the Republican establishment candidate, Governor Charlie Crist. Again, my colleagues scoffed because Rubio was 30 points behind in the polls. Then the SCF endorsed Rand Paul in Kentucky against the wishes of party leaders. After incumbent Republican Bob Bennett from Utah was tossed out by Tea Party activists, the SCF endorsed Mike Lee, a young constitutional conservative. They followed with an endorsement of businessman Ron Johnson against Russ Feingold in Wisconsin, another state where the so-called experts said a conservative couldn't win. But when the dust settled after the 2010 elections, all of these conservatives joined me in the Senate.

Americans proved they could take back their government. Republicans won a majority in the House of Representatives and gained seven seats in the Senate. But these victories only slowed the rampage of government spending and regulations by the Obama administration. Conservatives do not yet have the votes necessary to repeal the devastating policies enacted in the two years of total Democrat control. America remains on the verge of financial and cultural collapse.

Simply put, America may not survive another four years of President Obama and a Democrat-controlled Senate. This means 2012 may be our last chance to stop America's decline and turn things around. Freedom-loving Americans must be even more active in 2012 than in 2010. We must double our efforts, our numbers, and, hopefully, our victories.

This book will equip you with everything you need to know to help save our country. Please read it and share it with others, and join the fight for freedom.

I believe there are enough Americans who still consider this country worth saving. May we now join together for the fight of our lives—so that future generations can enjoy the blessings and prosperity provided by God and that have always defined this great land.

# 1

# America in Peril

# Introduction by Senator Pat Toomey

We stand at a crucial point in our nation's history. Too many for too long in our government have treated the wallets of American taxpayers like bottomless piggy banks, spending to their heart's desire. The result? A $15 trillion national debt, with many in government demanding that we keep borrowing and spending—and saying that the failure to do so would be "irresponsible."

Imagine a family that routinely lives beyond its means. That continuously spends more than they take in and makes up the difference by maxing out their credit cards. When this family reaches the limit on all of their credit cards—who would think it's a good idea to give them another credit card?

Such is the dangerous and dominant mind-set of Washington elites.

It's time for an honest debate on how we're going to get spending under control—a debate over what kind of spending cuts we must have and what kind of reforms we must make.

We can't just keep kicking the can down the road. We've been doing this for too long. It never ends well when government continues to take on too much debt, and nobody wants to see the government shut down. No one wants to see the disruption that might come from failing to raise the debt limit—again. Washington leaders are keen on reminding everyone on Capitol Hill about the supposed calamities that will occur if we stop borrowing and spending.

But they seem to forget what the American people want us to stop—a federal government that continues with business as usual.

When it comes to the economic crises we face—both today and in the future—there are two vital priorities that we need to focus on first and foremost here in Washington. The first is economic growth and the job creation that comes with it. The second is restoring fiscal discipline to a government that's lost all sense of fiscal discipline.

We can have terrific economic growth and the prosperity we've been looking for if the federal government would simply remember this—prosperity comes from the private sector. It doesn't come from government. The only help government can provide is improving the free market environment.

A well-functioning government does these four key things: First, it makes sure we have a legal system that respects property rights, because the clear title and ownership and ability to use private property are the cornerstone of a free enterprise system. Second, it requires that the government establish sensible regulations that are not excessive—too much regulation has unintended consequences that curb our ability to create the jobs that we need. Third, government needs to ensure a stable currency. We need sound money because debasing one's currency is the way to financial ruin—not the path to prosperity.

Fourth—and perhaps most important—governments need to live within their means. Government can't be spending too much money and can't have taxes at too high a level. Government spending must be limited, which means it should certainly be much less than what we have today.

On these four priorities the U.S. government is not doing a good job. The most egregious failure obviously continues to be the level of spending, and the Obama administration's spending alone amounts to about a 25 percent increase in the size of the government virtually overnight. Let me be clear— the federal government is now spending a quarter of America's entire economic output.

Our deficits are now over $1.5 trillion in a single year. That's more than 10 percent of our entire economy. And, of course, running up these annual deficits where we're spending more than we bring in—the shortfall is made up by borrowing from other nations like China to make up the difference. The size and scope of our debt is as overwhelming as it is alarming.

Such debt costs us job growth and jobs because it creates a tremendous uncertainty in our economic future due to an unsustainable fiscal path. This uncertainty discourages entrepreneurs and job creators from the kind of investment and entrepreneurial ingenuity we desperately need. The risks of doing nothing to change course are very real. History is replete with examples of countries that have accumulated too much debt, and it never ends well. Very often it leads to very high rates of inflation, and it can lead to much higher interest rates, which in turn can have a crippling effect on job growth. It also leads to financial disruptions, which can be very damaging as evidenced by recent events in Greece, Ireland, and elsewhere overseas.

The most irresponsible thing we could do is simply raise the debt limit and run up even more debt without doing anything to fix the problems that led to our current crisis. We need to have real cuts in spending now—not later, at some distant hypothetical point of time in the future—but now.

We need a balanced budget amendment. We need statutory spending caps written into law. We need to obey the Constitution again and get back to the spirit of our Founders: that of a free people who remain free due to a government that largely stays out of the way. Our government was supposed to be one that is severely limited—not one that diminishes citizens' prospects and darkens our children's future through unlimited spending and growth.

America can have a terrific economic recovery, booming growth, and tremendous job creation if government could once again help to create the right environment instead of hampering the individual and free market principles that have made this country great. If we can find the wisdom and will to do this, then the twenty-first century can be another great American century.

In 2008, candidate Barack Obama explained why he believed so many Americans were flocking to his presidential campaign:

"You did it because you know in your hearts that at this moment—a moment that will define a generation—we cannot afford to keep doing what we've been doing. We owe our children a better future. We owe our country a better future."

Candidate Obama won the last presidential election with many promises about what we owe this generation and the next. President Obama puts this country and its future in great peril precisely because of how much we now owe.

George W. Bush left this country with an $11 trillion national debt. Barack Obama has taken our debt to more than $15 trillion. According to the Bureau of Labor Statistics, in 2010 the share of our debt for each individual American worker was $90,962. Still, arguably the most heated debates in Washington today are over whether or not we should raise the legal debt limit or "debt ceiling." This is insanity.

Said candidate Obama: "Let us unite in common effort to chart a new course for America," and our President has done precisely this—by uniting the spending habits of the last administration with the even bigger government desires of his own.

Obama and his party have indeed charted a new course for America—off a cliff.

If yesterday's American family looked forward to a future of certain opportunity and prosperity, today's parents more often fear that there won't be any American dreams left for their own children—as we continue to borrow and print money as if there was no tomorrow. The Labor Bureau statistics that indicate that each individual American worker owes over $90,000 toward our debt also tell us each American family owes $10,807 to China alone. Why must the world's only superpower borrow from other nations to survive? Why is a country as great and wealthy as America so heavily indebted to China?

If something doesn't change quickly—there really will be no tomorrow. Unfortunately, many Americans have become immune to such telltale warnings.

Washington politicians have long used the word *crisis* to frighten and manipulate the public. During the 2008 bank bailouts, a Republican president insisted government had to act immediately to avoid economic calamity. In 2009, the Obama administration's stimulus spending was sold to the public with the same sense of urgency and impending doom. Many Americans were suspicious of these claims.

They were right to be suspicious.

We have become numb to politicians crying wolf when there is no wolf. We have grown weary of a government that always claims the sky is falling every time politicians need another excuse to spend to the moon. We've become fed up with Washington leaders who create a sense of panic in order to rush through some new government program—often to solve problems created by other government programs.

Alerting Americans to the current and very real threat of economic disaster will mean getting through to a general public that has become cynical and apathetic, and not without reason. Many Americans—and indeed much of the world—view the United States as being too big to fail. How could the world's largest economy collapse? We are the unsinkable *Titanic*!

Fortunately, many Americans—who understand full well what it's like to balance a checkbook or a household budget—can already see what so many Washington leaders can't: that the seemingly invincible United States is rapidly approaching an economic iceberg. Basic math tells us that we can't keep spending more than we are bringing in indefinitely.

Common sense tells us that America must reverse course.

The more we fully understand America's fiscal and economic crisis, the better equipped we'll be not only to address these problems but to enlist the support of those who truly understand what the situation demands. The most powerful message is the truth, and the worsening of our economic crisis can be avoided if we act.

But make no mistake. It really is now or never—and America literally cannot afford to ignore one of the most serious economic crises in the history of this great nation.

## Spending and Debt Are Out of Control

Washington always acts in great haste when it comes to spending money in the name of solving problems. But now it has become clear that our greatest problem is spending itself. Not surprisingly, Washington doesn't seem to be in any hurry to address it.

In 2011, health care, Social Security, and interest on the debt accounted for 50 percent of all federal spending. Defense represented 20 percent of total spending in 2011. All other spending represented 30 percent.

By 2021, health care and Social Security alone will require 50 percent of all federal spending. Interest on the national debt will increase to 16 percent of the budget (interest costs will be much more if interest rates return to historical norms). Defense and other spending, such as education, transportation, and welfare, will all decrease substantially.

The national debt is the total amount the United States owes. Our national deficit is the amount we owe or borrow annually. Since 2005 annual deficits have increased exponentially, reaching a $1.6 trillion deficit in 2011. This is the largest one-year deficit in American history, and the borrowing required for that year alone was larger than the entire federal budget only three decades ago.

This is not some temporary problem caused by the recession. The current projections indicate annual deficits will average nearly a trillion dollars for the next ten years. Unless immediate action is taken to reduce spending and to grow our economy, our debt will increase from $15 trillion to $25 trillion over the next ten years—even after the so-called historic spending cuts President Obama and some in Congress are crowing about. The only thing historic about the current reforms the Democrats have suggested is that they are the same ineffective proposals Washington politicians have promoted for most of our history—trying to convince voters that a decrease in new spending somehow constitutes an actual reduction in overall spending.

No serious observer believes America can handle this much debt, so something dramatic must now occur—for better or worse. Either Americans will elect a new president and new politicians serious about balancing our budget or there will be an economic apocalypse.

Once again, this is not hyperbole—it's basic math. Our current political leaders have proven time and again that they will not make the tough choices necessary to save this country. If this country is to avoid fiscal ruin, the ability to make tough choices must be voters' new litmus test—and the politicians unable to make those choices must be replaced!

## Debt Concerns Now Unify Americans

Even in confronting this unfortunate doom and gloom, there is a silver lining. Americans are perhaps more united than ever against irresponsible spending and debt. The Tea Party movement, though new and unorganized, stunned the Washington political establishment in the 2010 elections by throwing out the Democrat majority in the House and weakening the Democrat majority in the Senate. More than a few big-spending senior Republicans were also sent home.

Simply put, the Tea Party sees a more important dividing line than mere Republican versus Democrat—and supports only those who believe in limited government as opposed to the politicians in both parties who still consider government unlimited.

Millions of Americans who were fed up with a Republican president who doubled the size of government and the debt voted for "hope" and "change" in 2008. We then became stuck with a Democratic President who has now tripled the size of government and the debt—and he's just getting started.

In the last four years, Americans from across the political spectrum united in their opposition to ObamaCare, a big-government disaster that continues to prove even more devilish with every new detail. Tea Party members became alarmed and angry over the massive growth of government, exorbitant new spending programs, and the government takeover of private companies and the health-care industry. These grassroots activists were not just Republicans; they included Democrats, libertarians, independents, and many who had never been involved in politics. Americans from different backgrounds and political persuasions voiced grave concern over the troubling direction of their country. It was the beginning of an American awakening.

I was dubbed "Senator Tea Party" due to my vocal support for the many grassroots rallies organized throughout the country. When I spoke at Tea Party events and made my way through the crowds, I would often hear three things: *Thanks for fighting*, *Don't back down*, and *We're praying for you*. And of course everyone would ask, *What can we do?* These folks came from all walks of life, but they were all eager for political leadership from elected officials serious about stopping the federal government from bankrupting our nation.

While Congress and President Obama are deeply divided

over spending issues, Americans are increasingly unified over their demands for our government to live within its means and to balance the federal budget. Americans now overwhelmingly support a balanced budget amendment to the Constitution that would force the President and Congress to actually balance the federal budget every year. Passing a constitutional requirement to balance the federal budget should be any serious candidate's war cry as we head into the 2012 elections.

This would finally and permanently put a spending straitjacket on Washington politicians. As expected, congressional Democrats consistently block the passage of any legislation toward this end.

## Obama and the Democrats Are Not Serious about Debt

The resistance by President Obama and the Democrats to addressing our debt crisis was on full display during the 2011 budget debates. After more than two years of operating the federal government with no budget—and after watching Obama increase the federal debt by more than four trillion dollars—my frustration with the President and Democrat leadership had boiled over.

In one of my many speeches on the Senate floor attempting to sound the alarm to congressional colleagues and C-SPAN viewers, I used posters to make my points. My first poster was a quote from Obama when he was a Senator in 2006: "Increasing America's debt weakens us domestically and internationally." I also noted that Senator Obama accused President Bush of "a failure of leadership" for asking Congress to increase the federal government's debt ceiling. Now Obama and the Democrats not only chastise Republicans who refuse to raise the debt ceiling as irresponsible, but the President has asked Congress to increase our debt limit four times in his first three years as President.

The hypocrisy was astounding, the fiscal recklessness even more so.

I also used a poster on the Senate floor that featured a chart comparing America's national debt relative to the size of our economy to three bankrupt European nations (Greece, Ireland, and Portugal). These nations had already used emergency bailout funds to avoid defaulting on their loans. America's debt relative to the size of our economy is already greater than both Ireland and Portugal. Unlike these smaller countries, if America needed a bailout, there is no country or international organization that could rescue us.

Many Americans wonder how their government can so arrogantly and egregiously operate outside its budget. That's easy—there is no budget.

This is not a joke. Senate Democrats and the White House did not produce a budget for three years. Three years! How could we possibly get spending under control if we don't even have a budget? When President Obama finally did send a budget proposal to Congress in 2011, it almost doubled the national debt. Thankfully, the Senate voted it down 97–0. Lest anyone think I'm spinning some sort of partisan narrative to magnify this administration's glaring unconcern for our current crisis—not one Republican *or Democrat* voted for the President's 2011 budget. Not one. Even Obama's own party could not defend his indefensibly expensive budget.

That Majority Leader Harry Reid and Senate Democrats had not produced a budget of their own for three years was no surprise—budget plans reveal priorities, and the Democrats were afraid to show Americans their real plans. To illustrate this point,

I decided to put one of Senator Reid's quotes—which appeared in the *Los Angeles Times* on May 20, 2011—on a poster: "There's no need to have a Democratic budget...It would be foolish of us to do a budget at this stage." Reid was right. It would be foolish because it would reveal that the Democrats intended to raise taxes so they could continue to increase spending and expand government. Americans knew that we needed to cut spending, not raise taxes.

Apparently Reid and the Democrats planned to bank on the American people being foolish and apathetic. What faith they have in their fellow Americans!

## Republican Attempts to Cut Spending Met with Democrats' "Mediscare" Fearmongering

My Senate budget speech was part of the 2011 debate that led to four budget votes in the Senate. As mentioned earlier, one vote was on President Obama's proposed budget (defeated 97–0). Another vote was on Republican Senator Rand Paul's proposal to balance the budget within five years. Republicans also presented Senator Pat Toomey's proposal to balance the budget in ten years. Every Democrat voted against the President's budget and both of the Republican proposals.

Democrats also voted against the House Republican budget developed by Representative Paul Ryan, which included Medicare reforms. Senator Harry Reid forced a vote in the Senate because he believed that Democrats could use the Ryan budget and his suggested Medicare reforms to frighten senior citizens in the 2012 elections. Reid's confidence was buoyed by a special New York congressional election in 2011 that many pundits and observers believed was determined by the Medicare issue.

Democrats were ecstatic in May 2011 about their victory in New York's 26th District special election. This was one of the few congressional seats in New York that had been consistently held by Republicans. But after the Republican candidate expressed support for Ryan's Medicare reforms—and millions were spent on "Medi-scare" ads to frighten seniors—a Democrat won the seat.

One television commercial depicted an older woman in a wheelchair being thrown off a cliff with the message saying Republicans were going to destroy Medicare and leave seniors to die without health care.

Perhaps I'm just jaded or too cynical after working in Washington for twelve years—but I'm convinced Democrats believe Americans are stupid, especially seniors. And now Democratic strategists think they can win the 2012 elections by using misleading and dishonest information about Paul Ryan's plan to *save* Medicare.

The truth: the Democrats already have Medicare on a course for certain bankruptcy. They took a half trillion dollars from Medicare to help pay for ObamaCare while telling seniors that these cuts would somehow strengthen Medicare (remember: Democrats think we're stupid). And the President's 2011 budget cut Medicare payments to physicians another 35 percent.

Democrats plan on having a field day in 2012 by telling voters Republicans want to cut Medicare. Not only is this not true, it is ObamaCare that actually cuts Medicare.

The downward spiral of Medicare is becoming evident. Many

seniors are already having a difficult time finding doctors. Every year, fewer physicians accept new Medicare patients because government payments don't cover their costs. Medicare will soon pay doctors less than Medicaid, a health plan offered for the poor by the states. And these cuts in physician payments from Medicare are coming at a time when millions of baby boomers are reaching retirement. Anyone who believes Medicare can continue without reform is dreaming! Ryan's proposal does precisely this, and yet his plan to save Medicare has elicited only hysterics and scare tactics from the Democrats. Given Obama's budget, his party's lack of a budget in Congress, and the Democrats' general view of government as being unlimited and infinitely expandable, it's no secret which party continues to live in fantasyland.

The truth about the Ryan budget is this: it affects no one over fifty-five years old, but saves Medicare for current seniors by helping younger workers buy less expensive private health plans when they retire. This plan for younger workers will save money in the future, preserving traditional Medicare for everyone over fifty-five.

None of the changes envisioned by Ryan would take effect for ten years—so everyone over fifty-five will have traditional Medicare, and those who begin retiring in ten years will receive an annual subsidy from $8,000 to $12,000 to help pay for a personal health plan. An average of $10,000 is likely much more than most Americans pay for health care now annually. This is a plan that most retirees in the future will prefer because it will allow them to keep their private health plans and see the doctors of their choice.

## Health-Care Spending and Social Security Will Soon Consume the Entire Federal Budget

The Democrats' plan to use "Mediscare" tactics against Republicans in the 2012 elections is a sobering reminder of the utter lack of seriousness from Democrats when it comes to dealing with America's spending and debt. Federal spending impacts almost all areas of American life—but rapid increases in health-care spending are the greatest threat to American solvency.

Increases in Medicare costs alone are already crowding out other priorities like defense spending. When combined with all federal health-care spending and Social Security, entitlements will consume the entire federal budget in less than forty years. Democrats would have us believe that this is sustainable—basic math and common sense, however, prove otherwise.

Federal entitlements are growing rapidly and will soon crowd out other national priorities. And yet, President Obama and the Democrats have not proposed any reforms to slow the growth of these programs. In fact, they continue to propose new spending programs.

Federal health-care mandates are also forcing large spending increases upon the states. Medicaid, a state/federal health plan partnership for the poor, is pushing many states toward bankruptcy. Medicaid spending by states has increased four times faster than spending for elementary and secondary education, five times faster than higher education, and nine times faster than transportation spending over the past two decades.[1]

A block grant program for Medicaid would give states the opportunity to opt out of federal mandates and administer the program as they see fit. States that do this would be given a capped amount of money from the federal government to spend on the program. Rhode Island has already done this with success. Reports the *Wall Street Journal*: "Medicaid is the major cost driver in state budgets these days, so several Governors have proposed a deal to the White House and Congress: They'll take less money in return for the flexibility to run the program with fewer federal strings. A case study in the potential benefits is coming from liberal Rhode Island, of all unlikely places...In 2008, then-Governor Don Carcieri asked Washington for a Medicaid waiver and block grant to reform a program that consumed 30% of its budget...The results? After 18 months, Rhode Island's Medicaid spending, which was projected to reach $3.8 billion, has declined to $2.7 billion."

As Medicaid continues to consume a larger share of state budgets, new ObamaCare mandates require that by 2014, states must enroll every individual who resides in a household below 138 percent of the federal poverty level into Medicaid plans. Before ObamaCare was passed, a low income alone was not enough to qualify for Medicaid. The individual also had to meet other requirements that might include age, pregnancy, disability, or blindness. When ObamaCare becomes fully operational, Medicaid will be expanded to those who make below 138 percent of the poverty line. In 2011, the federal poverty line for a family of four is $22,250. When ObamaCare comes into effect, that poverty line is expected to be $33,000. This will increase the size of the welfare state by up to 25 million able-bodied adults.[2]

In addition to the growing pressure on state budgets, Obama-Care's expansion of Medicaid will likely lead to lower-quality health care. Only 10 percent of primary care physicians (PCPs) believe that new Medicaid enrollees will be able to find appropriate medical care after the expansion. Adding millions more individuals to Medicaid will likely cause a further deterioration in the quality of care Medicaid enrollees receive.[3]

Federal and state spending for health care will dwarf all other government spending—but Social Security will even further exacerbate our spending and debt problems. Social Security spending began to exceed projected tax collections in 2010, and these deficits will quickly grow to alarming proportions. After adjusting for inflation, annual deficits will reach $81.5 billion in 2020, $288.4 billion in 2030, and $343.6 billion in 2035.

Virtually every Democratic "reform" does nothing to address what is making entitlements insolvent while suggesting that we spend or borrow even more money—the very reason we are facing a financial crisis in the first place. Republicans are insisting that entitlements can be saved only by making tough and practical cost-cutting decisions. The Democrats seem to think Medicare, Medicaid, and Social Security can be saved through magic. Democrats continue to portray Republican attempts to reform entitlements as cutting or harming these programs—when in fact the persistent refusal to reform entitlements is the surest way to end them.

## Federal Regulations Cost Economy $1.75 Trillion Every Year

There are two sides to America's debt problem: spending and revenues. When American families face tough times they curtail spending. Common sense and math dictate that less revenue means sacrifices must be made—yet Washington continues to balk at this simple and obvious equation.

The federal government is obviously spending much more than we can afford. In fact, we are now irresponsibly borrowing 43 cents for every dollar we spend, with no way to pay it back. To make matters worse, America's exploding debt is compounded by the slow growth in tax revenues from a lethargic economy.

America's economy is burdened with federal policies that include the highest corporate tax rate in the world, unbridled litigation, and costly regulations. As government control has increased in almost every area of the American economy, the cost of regulation has slowed job growth and economic expansion. The federal government is making it increasingly difficult for American businesses to compete in the global economy.

The Small Business Administration's Office of Advocacy stated in September 2010: "The annual cost of federal regulations in the United States increased to more than $1.75 trillion in 2008. Had every U.S. household paid an equal share of the federal regulatory burden, each would have owed $15,586 in 2008."

And remember—this was before the recent further expansion of government that has coincided with the election of Barack Obama.

This expansion continues with no end in sight. Republicans often cite the absurd amount of government regulation that puts an unnecessary burden on small businesses. As the Obama administration promises more jobs it continues to make life difficult for those who do the hiring.

According to an August 2010 Heritage Foundation report:

"The Code of Federal Regulations, a compendium of all existing federal rules, hit a record high of 163,333 pages in 2009, an increase of some 22,000 since the beginning of the decade. One prime example of a major rule is the recent Environmental Protection Agency (EPA) final rule establishing a mandatory greenhouse gas emissions reporting program for sources with emissions that exceed 25,000 tons per year (74 Fed. Reg. 56,260). The EPA rule establishing mandatory greenhouse gas emissions reporting requirements is a huge burden to American businesses. Rules and regulations are not passed by Congress. They are unilaterally enacted by government agencies and unelected, unaccountable bureaucrats. The EPA example shows how just one rule can have devastating and costly effects—and the EPA estimates the cost of the rule at $115 million for the first year and $72 million on an annualized basis in subsequent years."

The Competitive Enterprise Institute's 2011 yearly report clearly shows how such regulation hurts American individuals and businesses. New jobs and any economic recovery that follows will naturally come from the private sector—precisely the folks the federal government now is trying to hamper even further. Concerning these regulations the CEI found: "Given 2010's actual government spending or outlays of $3.456 trillion, the regulatory 'hidden tax' [of $1.75 trillion] stands at an unprecedented 50.7 percent of the level of federal spending itself... Regulatory costs dwarf corporate income taxes of $157 billion [and are nearly double] the estimated 2010 individual income taxes of $936 billion... Combining regulatory costs with federal FY 2010 outlays of $3.456 trillion reveals a federal government whose share of the entire economy now reaches 35.5 percent."[4]

So with an American economy already heavily burdened by federal control and regulatory cost, President Obama's 2012 budget proposal, if enacted, would make it even harder for businesses to expand and add jobs.

Perhaps when the current administration talks about creating more jobs, it means employing more government employees and federal regulators.

Consider this—a report issued by the George Washington University Regulatory Studies Center and the Weidenbaum Center at Washington University in St. Louis found President Obama's proposed budget for Fiscal Year 2012 would increase regulatory costs by another $57.3 billion.[5]

Cumulatively, all of these numbers are indeed staggering. Yet few in Washington seem to possess the sense of urgency proportionate to what these troublesome statistics demand.

## Massive Debt Undermines Sound Monetary Policy

Another unaccountable, out-of-control arm of the federal government is the Federal Reserve. Republican Congressman Ron Paul has been warning about the dangers of the Fed for decades and continues to be a leading spokesman on this issue. In his book *Liberty Defined*, Paul gives a simple history of the Federal Reserve and notes the inherent dangers of the institution:

The problem is easily summarized. Money was once rooted in a scarce commodity like gold or silver. It could not be manufactured by governments. In the late eighteenth and in the nineteenth centuries, there were many

23

debates about the first and second Bank of the United States. In 1913, Congress created the Federal Reserve with the power to print new money. This allowed government to pay for wars and welfare, but it also generated economic instability with booms and busts...Since 1971, the dollar is not redeemable in anything but itself. It is nothing but a symbol, and there are no limits on the number of dollars government and the Fed can create. The result has been an unchecked expansion of the state and a brutal and long inflation that has reduced our living standards in deceptive ways.

Older Americans often wonder what happened to the days when you could go see a movie and enjoy popcorn and a soda for a quarter. This would be a minor and rather trivial example of one of the "deceptive" ways in which inflation spurred by the Federal Reserve has "reduced our living standards."

A less trivial but equally deceptive example would be what the Fed calls "quantitative easing," in which it simply prints more money out of thin air—devaluing our dollar and damaging our country's economic health and global standing. And in its role as a supposedly independent guardian of the dollar, the Federal Reserve has embarked on policies that have undermined worldwide confidence in our currency and set the stage for massive inflation.

The federal government's huge and growing debt has soaked up much of the available credit in America. This lack of capital in the private sector has slowed economic growth. The Federal Reserve responded to this credit crunch by buying much of the debt issued by the Treasury Department in 2010 and 2011. The honest term for this is "monetizing debt," but Chairman Ben Bernanke called it—you guessed it—"quantitative easing." Of course, both terms simply mean printing new money out of thin air. Since the beginning of 2011, the Fed's purchase of Treasury debt equals almost 90 percent of the increase in total public debt outstanding. The Federal Reserve has expanded America's money supply (printed money) at the fastest rate in history.[6] The dollar's current value when compared to gold, oil, and other commodities is now at an all-time low.[7] The result has been a loss of confidence in the dollar internationally, as evidenced by the drop in foreign-exchange transactions involving the U.S. dollar along with the decline in our currency's share of the makeup of global foreign-exchange reserves.[8] The International Monetary Fund has even considered replacements for the U.S. dollar as the world's reserve currency.[9]

The weakness of the dollar seriously complicates America's debt problems. If creditors like China believe the dollar will continue to lose value because of reckless monetary policies and the failure of Congress to control spending—they will either stop lending us money or significantly increase interest rates. Either outcome could be catastrophic because America is already backed into a corner: we are forced to borrow more money simply to pay our bills.

The creditworthiness of the United States is now in serious question. In April 2011, Standard & Poor's revised its out look on the nation's long-term credit rating from "stable" to "negative." This was a stunning slap in the face for the world's largest economy. S&P's report included the following statement:

We believe there is a material risk that U.S. policymakers might not reach an agreement on how to address medium- and long-term budgetary challenges by 2013; if an agreement is not reached and meaningful implementation does not begin by then, this would in our view render the U.S. fiscal profile meaningfully weaker than that of peer "AAA" sovereigns.... The U.S.'s fiscal profile has deteriorated steadily during the past decade and, in our view, has worsened further as a result of the recent financial crisis and ensuing recession. Moreover, more than two years after the beginning of the recent crisis, U.S. policymakers have still not agreed on a strategy to reverse recent fiscal deterioration or address longer-term fiscal pressures.

In 2003–2008, the U.S.'s general (total) government deficit fluctuated between 2% and 5% of GDP. Already noticeably larger than that of most "AAA" rated sovereigns, it ballooned to more than 11% in 2009 and has yet to recover.

In fact, in August 2011, Standard & Poor's downgraded America's rating, from "AAA" to "AA+."

Representative Ron Paul and I have pushed for an audit of the Federal Reserve to determine more about their policies and the worldwide scope of their operations. While we were able to pass a weak version of our audit bill, there is still much work to do. America's spending addiction, massive debt, paralyzing regulations on business, and reckless monetary policy have created the perfect storm for a worldwide economic apocalypse.

## Government Dependency Is Destroying Our
## Culture and Threatening Our Democracy

America's economic and fiscal situation is dire but it is solvable. Despite so many "expert" opinions to the contrary, spending can be controlled, our budget can be balanced, and monetary policy can be strengthened if there is the political will to do so. But Washington will continue to allow the nation to decline and even collapse before making the tough decisions necessary to turn things around—that is unless Americans finally demand action and elect people who are really willing to change things in Washington.

There is only one question that matters now: are there enough Americans who understand what needs to be done and are willing to do it?

We'll know the answer after the 2012 elections.

That said, too many Americans are dependent on the federal government for their jobs, income, health care, housing, food, and education. The Democrats have always known that a dependent voter is a dependable vote. Democracies become dysfunctional when too many voters expect more from government than it can dole out by taking from those who are actually producing wealth.

A June 2011 Gallup poll revealed the extent to which this mindset of dependency has taken hold in the American body politic:

> Americans break into two roughly evenly matched camps on the question of whether the government should enact heavy taxes on the rich to redistribute wealth in the U.S. Forty-seven percent believe the government should redistribute wealth in this way, while 49% disagree. . . .

27

While a solid majority of Americans, 57%, believe money and wealth in the U.S. should be more evenly distributed among the people, fewer than half favor using the federal tax code to do so. The fault line in these views is distinctly partisan, with most Democrats championing redistribution and most Republicans opposing it.

Dependency and the redistribution of wealth is precisely what got us into our current financial mess, and America is now close to the tipping point where more voters are receiving something from government than paying for government. Unfortunately, those who want more from government are better motivated and organized than those who actually pay for government, would like to keep more of the fruit of their labor, and want to live independently in what is supposed to be a free country.

We saw a microcosm of this in Wisconsin when union protesters clashed with Republicans after GOP Governor Scott Walker attempted to reform and reduce the state's budget. Walker was elected to tackle his state's budget, which necessarily meant having to confront sacred government spending cows—including exorbitant union benefits packages and collective bargaining powers that had helped to put taxpayers in debt. The Tea Party represents the first time in a long time that the overburdened taxpayer has had a voice—something often drowned out by those accustomed to getting whatever they want from government at any expense to their fellow Americans.

The Heritage Foundation produces an annual Dependency Index Report that measures the increase in the number of Americans who are dependent on the government. The 2010 report states:

> The number of Americans who pay taxes continues to shrink—and the United States is close to the point at which half of the population will not pay taxes for government benefits they receive. In 2009, 64.3 million Americans depended on the government...for their daily housing, food, and health care.

Social Security and Medicare force Americans of all income brackets into some level of government dependency. Public education, student loans, and scholarships trap parents and students into another form of dependency. Federal welfare programs subsidize unwed births, single parenthood, and often a lifetime of dependency for countless Americans. In trying to help single mothers left with the burden of raising a child on their own, government policies have encouraged women to stay single by giving them more money for doing so.

Such dependency often encourages other social problems. A *USA Today* editorial in 2011 reported that 41 percent of children born in the United States were born to unmarried mothers (up from 5 percent a half century ago, before welfare programs existed). That includes 73 percent of black children, 53 percent of Hispanic children, and 29 percent of white children. The editorial provided overwhelming evidence that children of single mothers—particularly teen mothers—suffer disproportionately high poverty rates, impaired development, and low school performance.[10]

Low school performance leads to high dropout rates by children raised by single mothers. Research by Cecilia Rouse, professor of economics and public affairs at Princeton University, shows that each dropout, over his or her lifetime, costs the nation approximately $260,000.[11]

Welfare programs have only served to subsidize the poverty problem, not cure it. Instead of alleviating poverty, welfare simply institutionalizes it. These programs are meant to help the poor but have trapped many people into a life of single-parenthood—which often results in more poverty. Most poor families in America are single-parent households. Seventy-one percent of poor families with children are headed by single parents. By contrast, 74 percent of all families with children above the poverty level are headed by married couples.[12]

As with Medicaid and other federal programs, the problems with welfare and public assistance could also be solved by giving such responsibilities back to the states. In my book *The Great American Awakening*, I proposed that we "phase out federal welfare programs, and give block grants to states to partner with churches and charitable groups to assist the poor. Use federal block grants to assist states in setting up safety net programs to provide support for poor and disabled citizens." Another costly societal ill caused in large part by perverse federal policies is drug use. Much of the sale and use of drugs occurs among school dropouts with low incomes from single-parent households. Estimates of the total overall costs of substance abuse in the United States, including productivity and health- and crime-related costs, exceed $600 billion annually. This includes approximately $181 billion for illicit drugs, $193 billion for tobacco, and $235 billion for alcohol.[13]

In total, the federal government spends more than $400 billion a year on welfare programs. The Heritage Foundation concludes: "The federal government operates over 70 means-tested welfare programs that provide cash, food, housing, medical care, and targeted social services to poor and low-income persons.[14] In fiscal year 2010, federal and state governments spent over $400 billion on means-tested welfare for low-income families with children. Roughly three-quarters of this welfare assistance, or $300 billion, went to single-parent families. Most non-marital births are currently paid for by the taxpayers through the Medicaid system, and a wide variety of welfare assistance will continue to be given to the mother and child for nearly two decades after the child is born."

The cost in dollars of federal entitlements and welfare is huge, but these costs are small in comparison to the overall price we pay for institutionalizing government dependency and continuing to damage Americans' traditional spirit of independence and individualism. The millions of Americans receiving benefits from the federal government are easily frightened and manipulated into voting for candidates who promise more from government. Those candidates and their unreasonable promises—which are always expanding—are what have contributed greatly to our current economic woes.

A record number of Americans—about 14 percent—now rely on the federal government's food stamps program. More than 44.5 million Americans received food stamps in March 2011, an 11 percent increase from one year ago and nearly 61 percent higher than the same time four years ago.[15] Many of these people will vote in 2012, but it is highly unlikely they will vote for a conservative who promises to cut government spending.

If spending is an addiction by Washington politicians, then dependent citizens are both their enablers and their victims. This cannot endure, because if this pattern continues this country will not endure—and we must enlist more independent, hardworking, and thoughtful citizens to help stop this insanity before it's too late.

## Share the Truth

- Republicans and Democrats have created unsustainable spending and debt levels for America.
- Government spending and borrowing are smothering private sector investment and growth.
- The Federal Reserve is printing money to buy government debt, threatening the confidence in the dollar around the world.
- Entitlement spending, especially for health care, will soon bankrupt America unless reforms are implemented. But Democrats use "Mediscare" campaigns to frighten seniors when Republicans suggest reforms.
- Nearly half of Americans are dependent on the government for their income, housing, food, or healthcare. And half of Americans pay no federal income tax. This makes it difficult to get a majority of citizens to vote for Republicans who support less spending and less government.
- Americans who are working and paying taxes must get more involved in the political process if we are going to save America from economic collapse.
- The future of America is in the hands of the people, not the politicians.

- America is in trouble and in imminent danger of economic and financial collapse.
- The spending and borrowing policies of the Obama administration and the Democratic Party are accelerating America's decline.
- The 2012 elections may be the last chance for citizens to save America with their voices and votes.
- Think positive: we can and will win!

*Now or Never* is your handbook to select and support the candidates who will stand with courage, conviction, and principles, and fight to take back our government.

# 2

# Remembering Why America Is Exceptional

## Introduction by Senator Marco Rubio

Since this country's earliest days, America has inspired people all over the world to come here to pursue their dreams, work hard, and make a brighter future for their children. This sort of inspiration cannot be found in all nations or even most nations.

But it is part of what defines us as Americans. While there have been many great countries in the past, how many were so bold as to declare themselves the "greatest country"? Very few that survived, anyway.

Yet for well over two hundred years, generations of Americans have proudly—and rightly—made this claim. This bold statement rings just as true today, and Americans remain just as great as we have ever been.

But the same cannot be said for our government.

Today, it is precisely our government that keeps getting in the way of America doing what it has always done better than anyone else: create jobs. If Washington could just agree on a plan to start getting our debt under control, if we could just make our tax code simpler and more predictable, and if we could just get the government to ease up on some of these onerous regulations—the American people will take care of the rest.

If we can give America a government that lives within its

means, our economy will give us a government whose means are considerable. We need a government that can afford to pay for the things government should do because it does not waste money on things it should not do.

The American story is not one of a nation that's never had problems. It is the story of a nation that has faced many challenges and solved them. Every single one of us is the descendant of a go-getter, of dreamers and believers, and of men and women who took risks and made sacrifices because they wanted to leave their children better off than themselves. Whether they came here on the *Mayflower*, on a slave ship, or on an airplane from Havana, we are all the descendants of the men and women who built the greatest nation in the history of the world despite the roughest hardships imaginable.

We still possess the ability to confront any challenge. The only thing standing in the way of solving today's problems is our willingness to do so.

I know this about Americans because my family has lived it. My grandfather was an enormous influence on me growing up. He was born in 1899 to a poor, rural family in Cuba. When he was a very young man he had polio and it permanently disabled him. Since he couldn't work the farm they sent him away to school. In fact, he became the only member of his family who could read—and he would read anything and everything he could.

When I was growing up my grandfather lived with us. And on many days I would sit on the porch of our home and listen to him tell me stories about history, about politics, and about baseball, as he puffed one of his three daily cigars.

It's been over twenty-seven years since I've sat on that porch, and all the details about what he told me are not as clear as they once were. But there's one thing I vividly remember. It was a powerful sentiment that he wanted to make sure I understood: that because of where he was born and who he was born to, there was only so much he was able to accomplish. But he wanted me to know that I would not have those limits, that there were no dreams, no ambitions, no aspirations, unavailable to me.

My grandfather was right. I was not born to a wealthy or connected family, and yet I have never felt limited by the circumstances of my birth. I have never once felt that there was something I couldn't do because of who my parents were or weren't.

Now, why is it that I've been able to accomplish the things that my grandfather could not? Why did my dreams have the chance that his didn't?

The answer is simple: because I *am* privileged. I am privileged to be a citizen of the single greatest society in all of human history. There's never been a nation like the United States, ever. It begins with the principles of our founding documents, which recognize that our rights come from God, not government.

These principles embody the commitment to individual liberty that has made us the freest people in history. They also made possible our free enterprise economy, which has made us the most prosperous people in history. The result is an America that is the only place in the world where it doesn't matter who your parents are or where you came from. You can be anything you are willing to work hard to be.

For many of us who were born and raised in this country, including me, it's sometimes easy to forget how special America really is. But I was raised by people who know what it is like to lose their country, by people who have a unique perspective on why elections (or lack thereof) matter, by people who clearly understand how different America is from the rest of the world.

They've taught me this my whole life.

And they taught me, by word and by deed, that what makes America great is not that we have more rich people than anybody else. What makes America great is that dreams that are impossible to fulfill everywhere else are possible here. And why is that? It's because of the choices made by the people who came before us.

Almost every other country in the world chose to have the government run the economy. They chose to allow government to decide which companies survive and fail. They chose to allow government to determine which industries are to be rewarded. But the problem is that when government controls the economy, those who can influence government keep winning, and everybody else just stays the same. And so in those countries, the employee never becomes the employer, the small business can never compete with a big business, and no matter how hard your parents work or how many sacrifices they make, if you weren't born into the right family in those countries, there's only so far you can go.

Now, we've had our excesses here in America, but for the better part of 235 years, Americans have chosen something very different. Americans chose individual liberty instead of the false security of government. Americans chose a limited government that exists to protect our rights, not to grant them.

Americans chose a free enterprise system designed to provide a quality of opportunity, not compel a quality of results.

The final verdict on our generation will be written by Americans who haven't even been born yet. Let us make sure they write that we made the right choice, that in the early years of this century, faced with troubling and uncertain times, there were those who believed that the great American story had run its course. But we did not agree. Fear did not lead us to abandon our liberty. Uncertainty did not lead us to abandon the entrepreneurial spirit. We fought for and held on to those things that made us exceptional.

And because we did, there was still one place in the world where the individual was more important than the state. Because we did, there was still at least one place in the world where who you come from does not determine where you get to go.

Because we did, America survived, thrived, and still stood tall as the greatest country the world has ever known.

Marco Rubio's explanation of what makes America exceptional is inspiring because his family has lived it. As the Senator also notes, the concept is nothing new.

For example, many believe the origins of American Exceptionalism are best depicted in the writings of Alexis de Tocqueville, the French aristocrat and intellectual whose 1835 book, *Democracy in America*, is the most respected analysis of early American life. Wrote de Tocqueville:

> The position of the Americans is therefore quite exceptional, and it may be believed that no democratic people will ever be placed in a similar one. Their strictly Puritanical origin—their exclusively commercial habits—even the country they inhabit...[The American's] passions, his wants, his education, and everything about him seem to unite in drawing the native of the United States

earthward; his religion alone bids him turn, from time to time, a transient and distracted glance to heaven.

Conservative author Russell Kirk described what he believed made this country unique in a 1957 book entitled *The American Cause*:

The American mission is not to make all the world one America, but rather to maintain America as a fortress of principle and in some respects an example to other nations. The American cause is not to stamp out of existence all rivals, but simply to keep alive the principles and institutions which have made the American nation great.

In his famous 1964 speech "A Time for Choosing," in support of Senator Barry Goldwater's presidential candidacy, Ronald Reagan gave us his view of America's exceptional nature and the grave importance of protecting what makes it special:

If we lose freedom here, there's no place to escape to. This is the last stand on earth. And this idea that government is beholden to the people, that it has no other source of power except the sovereign people, is still the newest and the most unique idea in all the long history of man's relation to man.

What Reagan said next could have just as easily applied to what we face in 2012:

This is the issue of this election: Whether we believe in our capacity for self-government or whether we abandon the American revolution and confess that a little intellectual elite in a far-distant capitol can plan our lives for us better than we can plan them ourselves.

One can imagine what Reagan would think of the spend-happy and micromanagerial "elite" in Washington today. When Reagan was elected in 1980, most Americans could look to a future in which their children would live better than their parents, and the national debt was less than a trillion dollars.

How times have changed. America is in serious trouble, and a large majority of voters believe Washington is making things worse by continuing to lead us in the *wrong* direction. But there is little consensus about what is the *right* direction. We are united around the need to cut government spending—but there is no agreement about what to cut. Some believe we should balance the federal budget by increasing taxes on those who create jobs and make over $200,000 a year.

Reagan might have been criticized often for doubling the national debt (due in large part to a Democrat-controlled Congress) from less than a trillion dollars to two trillion—but his successors have now taken it to over $15 trillion, with many in Washington now saying it would be "irresponsible" not to keep borrowing. Unlike the Reagan era, most Americans do not see a future in which their children will do better than they have. But today too many Americans aren't dreaming about the future—they're fearing it. Today, there is little agreement about anything in this country except this: we are going in the wrong direction.

While America does face serious challenges, any constructive discussion of these problems should begin with optimism. We should be optimistic because all of the positive factors that made our country great are still at work today—they have just been hindered heavily by an intrusive and overbearing government.

America is plentiful in its natural resources. The values and principles that made America exceptional are still working whenever and wherever they are allowed to work. We can solve our problems and put America back on the right track by remembering what made us great to begin with.

And we can start by trying to figure out where we took a wrong turn.

Much of the confusion and polarization in our politics today is because of the fact that few Americans know or understand the origins of our greatness and what makes our country truly exceptional. America really is unlike any other nation in history, and it is imperative that voters rediscover how and why this is true.

America became the most prosperous, the strongest, and the most compassionate nation in history because it originated as a decentralized and self-governing society—a society that put a high value on individualism, which drastically lessened the restrictions on social and economic mobility. Most other nations of a size and strength comparable to the United States originated from a centralized power structure featuring social caste systems. Such caste systems trapped citizens in socioeconomic groups with little hope of upward mobility.

Today's government-run public schools have done a poor job of teaching our students about America's uniqueness. Our liberal-controlled systems of higher education do not emphasize the differences or even attempt to illustrate the important implications of centralized versus decentralized political power.

Since many citizens don't consider what the federal government can accomplish versus what states and local communities can do better, many of today's political issues and public policies have become a confusing array of nonsensical and contradictory rhetoric to them. Politicians who claim to want to help "the little guy" often do so by promoting the transfer of wealth and power from states and cities, or families and individuals, to an ever-expanding central government. These damaging big-government ideas—in the name of supposedly good causes—have long corrupted our politics and confounded the average voter. Voters often have no point of reference from which to judge the merits of the policy differences between candidates and political parties.

It doesn't require four years at a conservative college to remind us of our forgotten history. A brief review of America's origins will quickly reveal how millions of individuals built our nation from the bottom up.

Freedom is what occurs when millions of people make their own decisions about what they value and what they do. America began as an experiment in freedom, and it is our characteristic reverence for liberty that has made us great. Returning to decentralized political power and individualism will restore freedom—and this restoration of freedom will help rebuild America's greatness.

## America—Free from the Beginning

Imagine for a moment the treacherous journey of our ancestors who left their lives and families behind in seventeenth- and eighteenth-century Europe. Those who boarded crowded ships for long and often dangerous voyages to the New World. So many pioneers and pilgrims came here only to live in crude and primitive settlements, often dying from the freezing cold or due to rampant disease. Most arrived with nothing more than the clothes on their backs. Only their hard work and resourcefulness would keep them alive.

Yet they came by the thousands, establishing small settlements along the east coast of this new land. Many risked their lives in order to escape religious, political, and economic tyranny. Some came as adventurers, opportunists, and profiteers—but all were brave souls who voluntarily ventured into an unknown and dangerous world in the hopes of finding freedom and opportunity.

Many historians prefer to avoid or downplay the fact that many of America's earliest settlers were motivated primarily by a quest for religious freedom. Many of today's intellectuals prefer to minimize the role of religion in America's founding. But there is no getting around the fact that the principles and values that made early America successful were derived largely from religious faith.

De Tocqueville wrote in 1835:

It was religion that gave birth to the English colonies in America. One must never forget that....I see the entire destiny of America embodied in the first Puritan to land on its shores, just as the entire human race was embodied in the first man.... Despotism can do without faith, but liberty cannot.... When a people's religion is destroyed... then not only will they let their freedom be taken from them, but often they actually hand it over themselves.[1]

Aside from the typical and obvious religious concerns of eternity and morality, religion in the early American colonies fulfilled an important temporal function by facilitating individualism and decentralization. Religion encouraged individual accountability and character traits that are essential to self-government: personal responsibility, self-restraint, commitment to family, charity, hard work, sacrifice, and delayed gratification.

This is likely what John Adams meant when he wrote: "Our Constitution was made only for a moral and religious people. It is wholly inadequate to the government of any other."

If Adams believed that America's religious character was the framework for constitutional government, Senator Rand Paul has noted that it is precisely the ideas of our Founding Fathers that make America exceptional. Wrote Paul in his book *The Tea Party Goes to Washington*:

America's exceptionalism, or specialness, is something that is enshrined in our documents, from the Declaration of Independence to the Constitution... How did America come to be the richest and freest nation know to history? America is exceptional, not inherently so, but because throughout our history, we embraced freedom. We fought for it. Men and women have died for it.

Paul added: "America will remain great if we remain proud of the American system, a system that enshrines and protects by law a system of free exchange or capitalism ..."

It is precisely the American system of free markets and individualism that is under attack today. This hasn't always been the case.

Technically, the American colonists lived under the rule of the King of England, but the large barrier of the Atlantic Ocean insulated them from the direct control of the King. Early Americans were generally free socially, economically, and politically. Free enterprise grew rapidly in settlements where most were entrepreneurs by necessity: farmers, merchants, trappers, shippers, inventors, and traders.

British economist Adam Smith confirmed the social and economic benefits of decentralization and individualism in *The Wealth of Nations*, published in 1776. Smith dispelled the myth that individual ambitions and pursuits were a detriment to the common good:

> The uniform, constant, and uninterrupted effort of every man to better his condition, the principle from which public and national, as well as private [wealth] is originally derived, is frequently powerful enough to maintain the natural progress of things toward improvement, in spite both of the extravagance of government, and of the greatest errors of administration.[2]

Later, Friedrich Hayek (1899–1992), the Nobel Prize–winning, Austrian-born economist, emphasized that the spontaneous and uncontrolled efforts of individuals were capable of producing a complex order of economic activities that could not be managed by a central authority. Socialists argue that the spontaneous economic activity inherent in a free market system produces inevitable inequities that consequently must be managed by government. But the socialists' argument ignores the historical evidence that central economic planning inevitably leads to economic stagnation and large-scale human suffering.[3] This is a lesson twentieth-century Europe, much of it under the spell of the collectivist ideologies of fascism or socialism, would learn the hard way.

Hayek argued that democracy and free enterprise were incompatible with societal management by government. Hayek quoted de Tocqueville to make this point:

Nobody saw more clearly than De Tocqueville that democracy as an essentially individualist institution stood in an irreconcilable conflict with socialism: "Democracy extends the sphere of individual freedom," he said in 1848, "socialism restricts it. Democracy attaches all possible value to each man; socialism makes each man a mere agent, a mere number. Democracy and socialism have nothing in common but one word: equality. But notice the difference: while democracy seeks equality in liberty, socialism seeks equality in restraint and servitude."[4]

The colonists experienced unprecedented levels of liberty many years before the Declaration of Independence and the Constitution—in fact those documents were a reflection of Americans' historic freedoms. Personal responsibility begat unprecedented personal autonomy. Hard work and sacrifice yielded levels of economic freedom and social mobility unimaginable in Europe. Few colonists became wealthy, and most survived with very modest means. But a strong prevailing sense of community and charity protected neighbors from destitution and isolation—*without* government intervention.

More by accident than design, these ingredients for a free society—as illustrated here by thinkers like de Tocqueville and Hayek—converged in the early American colonies. This was not the result of a particular form of government or any central plan of the political class. It was the result of the particular character of the men and women who were willing to sacrifice their lives for the opportunity to live free.

America became exceptional because it was founded by exceptional individuals.

## Competing Visions

While America was developing from decentralized economic, political, and societal structures, Europe continued its trend toward centralized power and collectivism. These competing visions can be traced to opposing views of human nature and the differing beliefs about how to harness that nature for the good of society.

The American vision was founded in the Judeo-Christian belief that mankind is inherently sinful and must be constrained internally by a fear of God and externally (as Adam Smith noted) by societal incentives that motivate people to improve themselves and serve the common good. The secular European vision was founded on the belief that mankind is inherently good and perfectible if society is properly planned and managed.

Of course any plan to organize society or "liberate" it from man's true nature would always require a powerful centralized government. Proponents of statism and centralized planning were plentiful, from the French Revolution, which saw man's inherent nature as an obstacle to true freedom ("Man was born free, and he is everywhere in chains," wrote the eighteenth-century philosopher Jean-Jacques Rousseau) to the ideologies of fascism and communism that would emerge and do so much damage in the 20th century.[5]

European nations in the eighteenth, nineteenth, and twentieth centuries developed out of these antireligious and progressive concepts. They promoted equality through centralization of power and universal social programs. Social justice meant that governments should orchestrate equitable circumstances and outcomes for all citizens. They assumed if everyone grew up and lived in the same environment, then the inherent goodness and virtue of mankind would prevail.

The American vision of societal organization reflected a totally different view of mankind. Adam Smith regarded human selfishness as a given. And he was not naïve about any inherent righteousness in economic capitalism. The capitalist's intentions were characterized by Smith as "mean rapacity," and he referred to capitalists as people who "seldom meet together, even for merriment or diversion, but the conversation ends in a conspiracy against the public, or in some contrivance to raise prices."[6]

Forcing profit seekers to compete for customers was the only practical way to force them to serve the interests of others and, at the same time, develop a vibrant and prosperous economy that served the interests of society as a whole. Edmund Burke, another prominent proponent of individualism and capitalism, concluded, "We cannot change the Nature of things and of men—but must act upon them the best we can."[7] Freedom operating within the constraints of law was the only rational way to deal with individuals whose natural tendencies were bent toward selfishness and corruption.

These competing visions of human nature and societal arrangements are at war in America today—and the progressive view that mankind is inherently virtuous is infinitely more attractive to the uninformed voter.

All of us would prefer to believe that our fellow sojourners on this earth are good people and that all evil is a result of unfortunate circumstances. It is tempting to believe that if government could provide everyone with comparable income, housing, food, clothes, education, and health care then societal ills would diminish and happiness would prevail. This is why progressives are hell-bent on centralized political power and universal services.

The Judeo-Christian view, which is essentially synonymous with today's conservative view (de Tocqueville, Smith, Hayek, and Burke have all been influential figures to generations of American conservatives), is that a decentralized societal structure based on individual rewards and punishment is the best way to harness the good and redirect the negative tendencies of human nature.

The superiority of the conservative view would soon be on full display as people began to compare the American and French revolutions.

## The American Vision Has Proved Superior

By the early 1700s, Americans had achieved a modest level of prosperity and security. Materialism and European rationalism began to chill the spiritual fervor that initially defined early colonists. But out of this state of spiritual decline and lethargy erupted one of the most powerful movements since the Reformation: the Great Awakening.[8]

The Great Awakening is credited by many historians with providing the spiritual inspiration and courage that led to America's demand for independence. It transformed lives, influenced society, and shaped the generation whose ideas and arms gave birth to our republic.[9] John Adams considered America's spiritual awakening to be the American Revolution:

> What do we mean by the American Revolution? Do we mean the American war? The Revolution was effected before the war commenced. The Revolution was in the minds and hearts of the people; a change in their religious sentiments of their duties and obligations.[10]

King George attempted to burden colonists with more regulations and taxes at the same time the Great Awakening was creating an outcry for more freedom. The legendary Boston Tea Party illustrated the growing contempt for English oppression. By 1776, Americans, much like the first settlers, risked their lives and fortunes for the cause of freedom when they declared independence from England.

The Revolutionary War was a battle between the decentralized forces of American minutemen and the world's most powerful centralized fighting force. There has never been a more unlikely military victory than America's humiliation of the British redcoats. But Americans won the long and costly war for independence and began the process of forming a more perfect union.

Unlike other revolutions in history, the American war for independence was fought for freedom, not centralized power. Other revolutions, such as the French Revolution of 1789 or the Russian Revolution of 1917, were all about power. As Alexander Hamilton observed during the bloodletting in Paris in the 1790s, "There is no real resemblance between what was the cause of America and what was the cause of France. The difference is no less great than that between liberty and licentiousness."[11] British statesman Edmund Burke was a supporter of the American Revolution and based his support on conservative principles. Burke's most famous book, *Reflections on the Revolution in France*, was a critique of that war as an effort to revolutionize human nature, a very anticonservative and progressive sentiment.

If progressive arguments for inherent human virtue were true, then those with absolute power would use their authority in ways that would benefit the masses. Instead, in both the French and Russian revolutions, small and ruthless groups seized the reins of power in the name of "the people." These fierce little factions overthrew the existing institutions of church and government, replacing them with atheistic dictatorships.[12] The results were not a display of human virtue—but a confirmation of the inherit sinfulness of mankind.

To maintain their iron-fisted grip on power, revolutionary leaders in France and Russia resorted to executions rather than elections. Forty thousand Frenchmen were beheaded during their revolution, most of them peasants. And the millions of Russians killed by Lenin and Stalin in their consolidation of power exceeded the combined death tolls of both world wars.[13]

Many liberals have noted that wars are often started in the name of religion. This is true. But it is also true that the twentieth century featured the bloodiest and most costly conflicts in human history—and those wars were started in the name of godless rationalism, whether in its fascist or communist forms.

The liberal, progressive dogma that now controls the Democratic Party is intent on purging religious principles and values from public policy debates. Their secular-socialist philosophy is fundamentally opposed to the vision that made America exceptional. An objective review will reveal that a large majority of the Democrats' policies move America toward centralized political power and universal government services, despite the tragic historical consequences of these policies in Europe, Russia, China, and around the world.

No government should promote any form of religion, but unless our elected leaders understand a biblical view of human nature supported by years of historical evidence, they will develop policies that are antithetical to American exceptionalism. Government planning or force has never yielded productivity and virtue from the people. Only accountability to God, economic necessity, and the rule of law can redirect the inherent negative tendencies of mankind toward morality, virtue, hard work, self-control, and personal responsibility.

These are the character traits that make people governable with only limited government and external control. This is what compels one neighbor to help another. And these are also the characteristics that provide some measure of restraint to elected leaders who are given the power to govern.

After Americans won their hard-fought war for independence, they were in no hurry to submit to a central power of their own making. Americans were innately suspicious of a central government, and all thirteen states insisted on a rigid compact—a constitution—that would severely limit the power of the new central government. So jealous they were of their liberties, the great debate between Alexander Hamilton's Federalists and Thomas Jefferson's Anti-Federalists was whether or not the Constitution might create too powerful a central government compared to the Articles of Confederation. To help ensure that this would not occur, Patrick Henry (decidedly in the Jefferson camp) insisted that a list of explicitly specific limits on the federal government be added.

These limits came in the form of ten amendments known as the Bill of Rights.

The American Constitution prescribed a republican form of government that protected the power and independence of the states while empowering a federal government to defend the states, maintain a stable currency, and promote interstate commerce.

The Constitution created a decentralized political system with power divided between the federal, state, and local governments. The federal government was also divided into three branches to further diffuse power and to assure checks and balances on federal power.

## America Divided: The Civil War

During the first half of the 1800s, America became the most dynamic, prosperous, and strongest nation in the world. The early constitutional republic was off and running. We were truly the land of freedom and opportunity. Courageous people from all around the world continued to risk their lives and fortunes to come to the United States.

Independent-minded immigrants continued to stock America with hardworking, moral individualists who came in search of better lives—except for an entire class of slave labor that was brought to America against their will. Slavery violated every principle of American greatness and was a cancer on all of our political, economic, and social institutions.

American states were divided between "free" and "slave" states, and this division expanded tensions and hostility between citizens in the north and south. By 1860, the tensions came to a boil, and America erupted into a horrible civil war that killed a half million people and maimed thousands more.

America paid a heavy and continuously compounding price for not ending slavery in a principled manner when our Constitution was written. Not only was the nation divided in war, many lives lost, and American wealth and power diminished, but political power became more centralized in Washington. Our decentralized republican form of government was weakened as more power shifted to the federal government during the war. And the resulting disabilities and poverty from the war led to the federal government's first entitlement programs in the form of veterans' pensions and disability benefits.

## The American Century

While the seeds of national central power were planted by the Civil War, America gradually recovered from the division and devastation of war by maintaining its original principles of individualism and decentralization. America's founding vision proved to be unequaled in all of history; the period between 1865 and 1965 was truly the American century.

Americans became legendary for their individualism and spirit of independence. We were known throughout the world as a culture of faith and character ("America is great because America is good," wrote de Tocqueville). Our free enterprise system left the government-controlled European economies in the dust. And America's political system, known for its decentralized balance of power between local, state, and federal government, proved eminently compatible with free people and a free economy.

America's poor and downtrodden were cared for by churches, religious organizations, and mutual aid societies with little government involvement. Volunteerism was the American way, and civic duty compelled Americans to serve their families, churches, and communities. De Tocqueville noted:

When a private individual meditates an undertaking, however directly connected it may be with the welfare of society, he never thinks of soliciting the co-operation of the government; but he publishes his plan, offers to execute it, courts the assistance of other individuals, and struggles manfully against all obstacles.[14]

America's free enterprise system and capitalist economy led the world in innovation and productivity. Practically every major invention—electricity, electric lighting, the telegraph, the telephone, steam engines, trains, automobiles, airplanes—were conceived of and commercialized in the United States. By 1950, the wealth and power of America was nothing short of stunning. As Andrew Bacevich notes in his book *The Limits of Power: The End of American Exceptionalism*:

> The country possessed nearly two-thirds of the world's gold reserves and more than half its entire manufacturing capacity. In 1947, the United States by itself accounted for one-third of world exports. Its foreign trade balance was comfortably in the black. As measured by value, its exports more than doubled its imports. The dollar had displaced the British pound sterling as the global reserve currency....Among the world's producers of oil, steel, airplanes, automobiles, and electronics, it ranked first in each category. In 1948, American per capita income exceeded by a factor of four the combined per capita income of Great Britain, France, West Germany, and Italy.[15]

America's economic and military power saved the world from tyranny in World War I and II, but as with the Civil War, these wars further centralized political and economic power in Washington and planted more seeds of centralization and collectivism.

And with this centralization and collectivism, America's

political leaders began to advocate a counterfeit vision, one opposed to the vision that made America exceptional. The unique qualities that have always defined this country have been seriously undermined by the destructive yet frustratingly steady path toward big government. Only by returning to our limited-government roots will America be able to finally return to some sense of constitutional and fiscal sanity.

## Share the Truth

- America is and has been from its inception a unique and exceptional nation.
- America is the greatest, most prosperous, most powerful, and most compassionate nation in the history of the world.
- America was founded with a unique vision of individualism and decentralized political, economic, and social authority rooted in Judeo-Christian values.
- The American vision proved superior to the centralization and collectivism of every other industrialized nation.
- The political polarization in America today is the result of two competing visions: individualism and decentralization versus collectivism and centralization.
- The modern-day Democratic Party has adopted the European vision of centralization and collectivism.

# 3

# The Philosophies and Policies That Changed America

# Introduction by Senator Mike Lee

America's founding generation understood the need for limited government, particularly at the national level. Having endured the tyranny of a large, all-powerful central government in far-off London—one that overtaxed citizens, regulated them too heavily, and was largely unconcerned with preserving their rights as British subjects—the Founders knew that government power must be kept in check. They believed that government should be divided, minimal, and kept as close to the people as practically possible.

After the Revolution, the Founders established a national government of explicit limited purpose with the Articles of Confederation. Under the Articles, the Congress's authority was sufficiently narrow, ensuring that American government would be managed primarily at the state and local levels, maximizing access and accountability.

However, our Founders soon recognized they had taken their local-government principles a bit too far. In their understandably jealous zeal to protect the former colonists from the kind of overreaching and oppressive national government they had just experienced, they created an extremely limited national government that was *too* weak to perform essential duties that properly belong at the federal level. For example, although

Congress was nominally empowered under the Articles to provide for America's national defense, it had no effective means of raising revenue to provide for that defense. Meanwhile, Congress was powerless to address regulation of interstate and foreign trade, another proper federal concern. Aware of the Articles' deficiencies, the Founders convened in Philadelphia during the summer of 1787, ostensibly to amend the existing governmental charter. However, by the time they adjourned, the delegates to the convention had drafted and signed their names to an entirely new document—the U.S. Constitution.

The Constitution did nothing to abandon the widely shared consensus that our national government should be vested only with limited and enumerated powers. In fact, it explicitly preserved that understanding. But at the same time, the Constitution authorized Congress to perform a series of functions—most of which are outlined in Article I, Section 8—that are distinctly national in character. These functions included regulating commerce (i.e., trade) between the states and with foreign nations, providing for national defense, declaring war, setting rules to govern naturalization, establishing a system of bankruptcy laws, adopting a uniform system of weights and measures, and enacting laws to protect trademarks, copyrights, and patents. But there was not—and to this day there still is not—any provision authorizing Congress to simply pass any law it sees fit.

Unlike legislative bodies in other countries, Congress does not have a general-purpose license to legislate for the "good of the public"; it must act pursuant to an affirmative constitutional grant of authority. In other words, Congress lacks what jurists and political scientists characterize as "general police powers." And it lacks such powers by explicit design.

This original understanding was reverently observed for nearly a century and a half. While debates arose from time to time regarding the precise contours of this or that power, or particular functions of Congress, national leaders typically honored the limited nature of their authority. Generally speaking, Congress did not attempt to push the envelope by passing legislation of dubious constitutional validity. In fact, it was more common for presidents and members of Congress to regularly oppose proposed federal legislation on the grounds that it exceeded the national government's limited authority as designated by the Constitution.

This limited-purpose understanding began to crumble during the era of the New Deal, when President Franklin D. Roosevelt, aided by his party's substantial majority in both houses of Congress, undertook an unprecedented effort to expand the size and scope of the federal government. FDR and Congress began passing legislation regulating distinctly local activities—including areas like labor, manufacturing, mining, and agriculture—all of which were historically regulated at the state and local level. The Supreme Court initially resisted this effort, insisting in several cases that the Constitution means what it says when it characterizes Congress's authority as limited, and that the power to regulate interstate commerce *does not* extend to every activity that can fairly be defined as commercial.

Frustrated by the Court's resistance to popular efforts to expand the role of the federal government, FDR and some members of Congress placed intense pressure on the Court. Among other things, they threatened to pass legislation (1) authorizing FDR to appoint several new justices, and (2) mandating the early retirement of several of the sitting justices who were perceived as most hostile to the New Deal approach.

Some have said that these threats had their intended effect. In April 1937, the Supreme Court broadened its approach and upheld Congress's effort to regulate labor relations in *National Labor Relations Board v. Jones & Laughlin Steel Corp.*, 301 U.S. 1 (1937). This new approach, which the Court clarified and expanded five years later in *Wickard v. Filburn*, 317 U.S. 111 (1942), established that Congress may regulate virtually any activity that has a substantial effect on interstate commerce. Translation: the courts will essentially leave Congress alone—giving federal legislators the liberty to determine and police the extent of their own powers. So long as Congress uttered the appropriate "magic words" and identified at least a tenuous connection between the regulated activity and interstate commerce, which it could almost always do, the New Deal–era courts allowed the Constitution to be turned on its head.

Guided by this exceedingly permissive standard, which remains in effect to this day, Congress has been steadily expanding the scope of its authority since 1937. So much for constitutionally limited government.

For a variety of reasons, the Supreme Court is unlikely to retreat from this standard. We therefore cannot rely on the Supreme Court to restore a constitutional form of government to America. But fortunately, there is another way of recovering what has been lost.

Restoring constitutionally limited government must, I believe, be accomplished through the political process and not through the courts. The Constitution, which requires every member of Congress to take an oath to uphold it, still grants that body only limited and enumerated powers. The fact that federal courts have been disinclined to enforce that obligation since 1937 does not mean that the requirement no longer exists. Instead, it means that the extent of Congress's power must be the subject of political debate and discussion.

Yet, such debate and discussion is unlikely to occur in Congress until voters demand it. Since the late 1930s, most voters have stopped short of insisting that this "constitutional debate" occur in Congress. But this is starting to change. Perhaps more than at any time since the New Deal era, voters are becoming increasingly concerned about the seemingly limitless power of Congress. Voters are beginning to place a premium on a candidate's willingness to oppose legislation that—regardless of each proposal's relative policy merits, and regardless of what the Supreme Court has been willing to tolerate—does not fit comfortably within the proper parameters of the Founders' general understanding of the Constitution.

If this trend continues to develop, and voters come together en masse to stand up for their constitutional heritage, we can gradually reclaim the truly limited government our Founders fought a revolution to win, and that they originally intended to be Americans' birthright.

America now dangles on the edge of a fiscal and economic cliff. We have changed our original vision from an individualistic and decentralized society to a collectivist and centralized political structure rife with waste and corruption. Federal policies now have the government owning or controlling a large and unprecedented part of America's economic activity—a condition more akin to socialism than capitalism.

The more we learn and assess, the more disturbing it gets!

Consider this: the federal government is now the nation's largest property owner (Washington holds the deed to nearly one-third of America's total landmass). By taxing us, our government "owns" over one-third of the profits of all businesses and more than one-third of the incomes of most working Americans. Washington controls and restricts the development of America's energy resources. Government controls the majority of education and health-care services in America. It owns the primary retirement income plan for most Americans (Social Security). And government—through a burdensome regulatory system and direct interventions into the financial markets—effectively controls a significant portion of the nation's economic development and business activity.[1]

How did this happen? How did America change so quickly from the "shining city upon a hill," the beacon of individual freedom, and the world's model for free enterprise economic prosperity to a nation on the brink of economic collapse?

The siren song of socialism that has lured Europe and almost every other nation in history now has America in its trance. Political salesmen for collectivism are irresistible; their pitch is always more attractive to uninformed voters. Economist Milton Friedman explains:

> The argument for collectivism, for government doing something, is simple. Anybody can understand it. "If there's something wrong, pass a law. If somebody is in trouble, get Mr. X to help them out." The argument for voluntary cooperation, for a free market, is not nearly so simple. It says, "You know, if you allow people to cooperate voluntarily and don't interfere with them, indirectly, through the operation of the market, they will improve matters more than you can improve it directly by appointing somebody." That's a subtle argument, and it's hard for people to understand. Moreover, people think that when you argue that way you're arguing for selfishness, for greed. That's utter nonsense.[2]

Unlike America's Founders, who understood well the dangers of centralized power, today's voters are not as familiar with these lessons of history. Being less suspicious of centralization than earlier generations makes the average voter more susceptible to the utopian promises of big government. Politicians understand this and exploit citizens' fear and insecurity—typically born of Washington's numerous contrived crises—to herd the masses into more dependency on big-government programs.

If Americans are convinced they are unable to survive and succeed on their own, they will demand that big government protect them and make them more secure. It was Benjamin Franklin who told us that any society that gives up liberty to gain security will deserve neither and lose both. Losing individual autonomy and drive kills the soul and diminishes the individual initiative required to build strong nations.

Collectivism is anathema to freedom and prosperity. All initiative, creativity, innovation, entrepreneurship, productivity, faith, love, and charity begin at the individual level. The philosophies and policies that have imperiled America are those that have diminished individualism while centralizing federal power and forcing citizens into dependency on collectivist government programs.

What makes America exceptional is the individual spirit—what makes us less exceptional is when we damage this important philosophical heritage.

## The Philosophies That Changed America

For nearly a hundred years prior to the Civil War, the United States resisted the European trend toward socialized economies, large central governments, and collectivist social programs. But the destruction and human tragedy of the Civil War led to federal actions that planted the seeds for more centralized federal power.

As most Americans know, the Civil War started in 1861. That was also the year of the first American income tax. To start, Congress placed a flat 3 percent tax on all incomes over $800, but later modified it to include a graduated tax. The Civil War also precipitated the first national pension program to assist poor and disabled veterans. Congress later repealed the income tax in 1872, but the seeds of federal entitlements and the ease of paying for them with an income tax had set the stage for the unrestricted expansion of the federal government in the future.[3]

A mere century after America declared her independence from an oppressive government in far-off England, the seeds of dependence on big government at home were already being planted.

In 1894, as part of a tariff bill, Congress once again enacted a 2 percent tax on annual income over $4,000. But the tax was immediately struck down by a 5–4 decision of the Supreme Court. This new interpretation by the Court—that an income tax was unconstitutional—created an obstacle for a growing European-style "enlightened" progressive movement in America. Progressives knew that centralized, so-called progressive policies would fail unless the federal government had the ability to tax personal income and business profits. The Founders intended for American government to be limited. To be more like the Europeans, progressives knew it must be virtually unlimited.

The progressive dream of limitless federal spending was soon accomplished with the Sixteenth Amendment to the Constitution, which allowed a federal income tax. An unlikely chain of events caused this to happen with the unwitting assistance of conservatives in Congress. As written in the *Milestones Documents* in the National Archives:

> The Democratic Party Platforms under the leadership of three-time Presidential candidate William Jennings Bryan, however, consistently included an income tax plank, and the progressive wing of the Republican Party also espoused the concept.
>
> In 1909 progressives in Congress again attached a provision for an income tax to a tariff bill. Conservatives, hoping to kill the idea for good, proposed a constitutional amendment enacting such a tax; they believed an amendment would never receive ratification by three-fourths of the states. Much to their surprise, the amendment was ratified by one state legislature after another, and on February 25, 1913, with the certification by Secretary of State Philander C. Knox, the 16th amendment took effect. Yet in 1913, due to generous exemptions and deductions, less than 1 percent of the population paid income taxes at the rate of only 1 percent of net income.
>
> This document settled the constitutional question of how to tax income and, by so doing, effected dramatic changes in the American way of life.[4]

Before the income tax, the federal government was limited to transactional taxes derived from tariffs, excise, and sales. These taxes were generally visible to the public because everyone paid them—and this visibility in turn made any tax increases susceptible to significant public resistance. Transparency meant the revenue raised to fund the federal government was limited— which in turn kept the role of the federal government equally limited. This was how the Founders' system was supposed to work.

But with the advent of the income tax, federal politicians were given almost unlimited power to spend and grow government. It effectively gave the federal government an ownership share in every citizen's labor and a percentage of the profits from the entire American economy. Such levels of government intrusion would've been beyond the wildest big government dreams of King George III.

Proponents of the income tax promised that the tax would never exceed 1 or 2 percent of income, but as is typically the case with politicians' promises, this soon changed. It wasn't long before Congress began to raise taxes on businesses and upper-income workers. This kept the political backlash to a minimum, since most workers did not see their taxes increase. This practice also gave birth to the often immoral and duplicitous use of class warfare strategies employed ad nauseam by progressives who pit different segments of society against each other for their own political gain. Sadly, this rhetoric continues to be front and center in so many political debates today.

The income tax and World War I (1914–1918) were catalysts for the growth of federal power, and they facilitated the initial successes of progressive philosophy in America. Not surprisingly, the implementation of the income tax and World War I coincided with America's first progressive president. President Woodrow Wilson (1913–1921) was the first American president to actively work against our original, decentralized, republican form of government. He started the modern practice of disregarding the Constitution for his own political ends.

Fox News legal analyst and television host Andrew Napolitano explains how Wilson's progressive legacy has contributed to our current economic crisis as it relates to the abuses of the Federal Reserve: "Since World War I, since the advent of the Federal Reserve, since the presidency of Woodrow Wilson, the federal government has never been out of debt, and it has never wanted to be. Prior to the Wilson era, when the government borrowed money, it paid it back ... It was truly a pernicious time for freedom. But free money is what Wilson left to his successors, and they all were seduced by it."

Napolitano adds: "The Constitution states that the Congress shall coin money and determine the value of it. For the first 125 years of the nation, that's what the Congress did. But Wilson persuaded Congress a hundred years ago to give that power away to a private bank—the Federal Reserve; thereby letting the bankers who ran it, not Congress and not the free market, determine the value of money. And these bankers, who became fabulously rich by doing this, appealed to the weakness in every president from President Wilson to President Obama—free money."

Once again, for progressives, unlimited government and having the unlimited power to tax and spend is a necessity.

Similar to many European secularists, Wilson was heavily influenced by Charles Darwin and believed that governments, like humans, must constantly evolve. He opposed the "Newtonian" view—similar to the law of gravity theorized by Sir Isaac Newton—that government should have an unchanging constitutional foundation. President Wilson argued that government should be "accountable to Darwin, not to Newton. It is modified by its environment, necessitated by its tasks, shaped to its functions by the sheer pressure of life.... Living political constitutions must be Darwinian in structure and in practice." In other words, the Constitution should mean simply whatever Wilson and his fellow progressives think it should mean—a concept President Obama and his party would readily recognize today.

This progressive and supposedly evolutionary thinking began to untie the moorings of constitutional limited government in America during Wilson's presidency, and it fed a growing secularist movement that affected every area of American life. Sociologist and author Marvin Olasky writes:

> Evolutionary thinking influenced not only Social Darwinists but socialists like H. G. Wells who thought it was time to advance beyond competitive enterprise. (Karl Marx in *Das Kapital* called Darwin's theory "epoch making" and told Friedrich Engels that *On the Origin of Species* "contains the basis in natural history for our view.") Many books and articles have linked Darwin's thought to Lenin, Stalin, Mao Tse-Tung, and Hitler: Darwin is obviously not responsible for the atrocities committed in his name, but evolutionary theory plus his musings about superior and inferior races provided a logical justification for anti-Semites and racists.[5]

Though secular-socialist philosophies began to take hold among political and academic elites in the early 1900s, this new thinking did not begin to significantly shape political policies until World War II and the decade-long Great Depression (1929–1940) frightened Americans into the arms of the federal government. The Great Depression shook America's confidence in individualism and free market capitalism.

So of course politicians were quick to come to the rescue.

Despite populist fears about capitalism that were often fed by progressive rhetoric, the Great Depression was more likely caused by protectionist trade policies and the mismanagement of our currency by the newly formed Federal Reserve—printing "free money," for example, as Napolitano explained—not by a failure of the free market. But politicians are loath to allow any crisis to pass without using it as an excuse to grow government. The Washington political class and the media convinced the American people that the Depression was caused by greedy corporations and a lack of federal control.

This should sound familiar. Today we hear that the housing bubble and current economic crisis were caused by too little government regulation—completely ignoring the Federal Reserve's complicity in artificially lowering the interest rate, thus allowing people who could not afford homes to buy them. "Greedy" capitalists took advantage of a situation created in large part by the government—which we are now supposed to believe can be solved by even more government intervention. Thomas Woods, author of *Meltdown: A Free Market Look at Why the Stock Market Collapsed, the Economy Tanked and Government Bailouts Make Things Worse*, writes: "As several economists have noted, blaming the crisis on greed is like blaming plane crashes on gravity." Woods also notes that through the Federal Reserve there "were more dollars being created between 2000 and 2007 than in the rest of the republic's history."

President Franklin D. Roosevelt used the "crises" of the Great Depression and World War II to move America toward European collectivist social policies. The American worldview changed dramatically during this unprecedented era of government expansion. FDR's successor, Harry Truman, inherited a nation with an outlook very different from our Founders. This was the pivotal point in American history, when we took a sharp left turn from a free republic and headed down the road toward a social democracy.[6]

Conservative author Andrew J. Bacevich explains the political shift that occurred under Wilson and Roosevelt and how American government was significantly transformed post-Truman: "FDR's predecessors had presided over a republic. Central to the functioning of that republic was a set of checks and balances designed to limit the concentration of political power. Truman's successors presided over a system defined by the concentration of power in Washington and, within Washington, in the executive branch."[7]

Bacevich has noted that these vast expansions of centralized government power coincided with some of the most significant wars in American history (the Civil War, World Wars I and II). As FDR would state bluntly, "War costs money." The dominant trend among conservatives in the early twentieth century was to oppose massive foreign interventions due in large part to a recognition of the centralizing effect of wartime politics and economics. This was the same reason the Founders so vigorously opposed America becoming involved in "entangling alliances." In retrospect, we now know defeating fascism and communism was the right thing to do, but the correlation between war and big government is certainly as true as the Founders once warned.

True to his progressive form, President Wilson would say that America went to war to "make the world safe for democracy," while, perhaps ironically, doing great damage to our republic at home. The most high-profile conservative politician of his time, Senator Robert Taft—known as "Mr. Republican"—had a much different, and much more sober, take on our two world wars. Taft, known as the most vigorous opponent in Washington of Wilson and FDR's progressive policies, rebuked Wilson's progressive foreign policy vision in 1946, saying we went to war "to maintain the freedom of our own people...Certainly we did not go to war to reform the world."

## The Policies That Changed America

No doubt much of the big government that became a permanent part of American life during the early to mid-twentieth century was created or supported for purportedly benevolent reasons, especially after the Great Depression. Still, there can be many pitfalls to good intentions, with which the path to hell is so often paved. In the name of ultimately helping his fellow Americans, FDR would radically alter the limited form of government established by their ancestors. FDR significantly expanded the power of unions, created a national pension plan (Social Security), and expanded welfare programs for the poor. Unions were synonymous with collectivism and central power, and FDR's actions created a permanent alliance between union bosses and the Democratic Party at the expense of American taxpayers.

Roosevelt's New Deal heralded a new era of unconstitutional and expansive centralization of power, using—you guessed it—various crises as an excuse. Writes Bacevich: "Since 1940, a succession of national security emergencies, real and imagined, have permitted the federal government to assume a vast array of new responsibilities at the expense of state and local authorities." Bacevich also notes how FDR's big-government legacy endures to this day, beginning with the New Deal: "The practice of citing national emergencies as a rationale for enhancing executive power began in earnest on March 6, 1933. On that date, two days after becoming President, Franklin D. Roosevelt issued a proclamation declaring a state of national emergency and ordering a bank holiday, thereby inaugurating the New Deal."

Bacevich adds: "The U.S. government has operated in a condition defined by emergency ever since."

As part of the New Deal, the concept of Social Security came about. Social Security was originally intended to be a safety net against poverty for older Americans. When it was created, workers and employers each paid 1 percent of the first $3,000 of a worker's salary (a maximum of $30 per year for workers). Today, Social Security is the largest tax paid by many Americans (a combined employee/employer contribution of 12.4 percent of the first $106,800 of wages paid). Today, the federal government automatically puts all of the money that should be set aside for the Social Security Trust Fund into the General Fund. If the revenue coming in via Social Security was responsibly set aside like it should be, our national debt would actually be much higher. Raiding the Social Security Trust Fund was a precedent set in 1968 by another progressive president, Lyndon B. Johnson, to help pay for the

Vietnam War. To date, the federal government has borrowed over $2 trillion from the Social Security Trust Fund to spend on other programs.

Contrary to what many Americans believe and what progressives love to say, there is no money in the Trust Fund to pay future benefits. Furthermore, the fundamentally flawed program faces a severe demographic crisis as members of the baby boom generation begin to retire. The mess we face with Social Security, a program so many are now dependent upon, is yet another example of a failed progressive policy, where the potential for unintended consequences was ignored at the program's inception.

Progressive, collectivist policies similar to Social Security continued to explode after FDR. In 1952, President Dwight Eisenhower created the Department of Transportation to build a national interstate highway system. Today, the U.S. DOT takes 18 cents in taxes from every gallon of gasoline and regulates the construction (promoting union labor) for local and state roads and bridges. Despite the exponential increase in spending by the federal Department of Transportation, America's infrastructure is deteriorating, proving yet again that the amount of money spent by the federal government does not translate into positive results.

The growth of bureaucracy and centralization of power would continue under Eisenhower, as Wilson and FDR had set a big-government precedent that became the new norm in Washington, D.C. Barack Obama is unquestionably the most big-government president to date—but it was the steady work of statist politicians and presidents in both parties that brought America to its current crisis.

In the 1960s, President Johnson—the aforementioned heir

to FDR's New Deal—created Medicare and expanded welfare programs to an even more destructive level through his vision of a government-managed "Great Society." For example, Medicare was initially intended to be a safety net for poor seniors who needed health care. Today, it is the only health plan available to most seniors because the government has squeezed private alternatives out of the system. Now, Medicare is trillions of dollars in debt, and there is no feasible way for the federal government to pay promised benefits to seniors. Also, little competition exists to fill the gap because of government's monopoly in the field of seniors' health.

After Johnson, President Richard Nixon created the Environmental Protection Agency to reduce pollution in the nation's air and water. The EPA served an important function, but like most federal agencies, it has grown far beyond its original mission (do you see a pattern here?). Today, the EPA imposes onerous regulations on almost every business sector, and these policies, largely based on projections of worst-case scenarios rather than reality, cost the economy hundreds of jobs and billions of dollars every year.

In the 1970s, President Jimmy Carter created the Department of Education to centralize control of public education in Washington. At the time, American students were the best and brightest in the world. Today, Americans spend more on education than any other nation, and our students are near the bottom when compared with the rest of the world. Liberal politicians continue to argue that we must spend more on education even as student performance declines in correlation with the further expansion of the education bureaucracy jealously protected by Washington leaders and teachers' unions. President Obama and the Democrats constantly stress that we can't give up on education—as if the federal government has done anything but make things worse, for decades, in terms of actually helping and better preparing American students for the future.

President Ronald Reagan slowed the growth of centralized federal power, lowered taxes, reduced regulations, and strengthened our military. His policies encouraged investment, innovation, and economic growth. The conservative Reagan Revolution spurred twenty years of economic growth, but President Bill Clinton's massive tax increases in the 1990s eventually grew the government and slowed economic growth. Many like to give Clinton credit for delivering the last balanced budget Washington has seen—something that had much to do with the Republican "revolution" in which the GOP retook Congress during the 1994 midterm elections—but once again, like every president since Wilson and FDR, Clinton left the federal government much larger than he found it.

Clinton's successor, President George W. Bush, also drastically increased the size of government with the largest entitlement expansion since Johnson, with Medicare Plan D and his doubling of the Department of Education with No Child Left Behind. Bush also inherited a recession, and his tax cuts would stimulate an economic recovery until the housing boom busted near the end of his presidency. The housing bubble was caused by easy credit and loose monetary policy and made worse by quasi-federal agencies created by congress: Fannie Mae and Freddie Mac. These two unaccountable behemoths packaged subprime mortgages (loans people couldn't afford to pay back) into investment securities and sold them around the world. When these securities lost value as housing prices plummeted, the world's financial system came unglued.

The financial crisis peaked as Bush was replaced by President Barack Obama. Like the Great Depression, the great recession was blamed on Wall Street and corporate greed. And like the Great Depression, the great recession was actually caused by an incompetent federal government and Federal Reserve.

President Obama, like many of his predecessors, used the financial crisis and ensuing recession to expand the power of the federal government. The bank bailouts were used as an excuse to pass the Dodd-Frank financial reform package that gave the federal government effective control over America's banking and financial system. This gave politicians indirect control over all economic activity in America, and things have only gotten worse since, following the same pattern that has been repeating itself since the inception of the progressive movement in America.

Obama also used the recession and resulting increase in the number of Americans without health insurance to nationalize America's health-care system. He and a supermajority of Democrats in Congress passed ObamaCare without one Republican vote. At a time when Americans fear a national debt that is already $15 trillion and rising, the Democrats saw fit to enact government health care to the tune of almost $1 trillion. And that is just the Democrats' estimate—as history has shown, virtually every government program always ends up costing much more than the so-called experts originally planned.

Few Americans are even aware that for most of our history, the federal government had little or no role in education, health care, transportation, energy production, banking and investments, and retirement pensions. None of these activities are authorized by the Constitution as functions of the federal government. While the federal government should facilitate constructive action in all of these areas, they have proved ineffective, wasteful, and incompetent at managing these functions.

Numerous Supreme Court decisions over the past sixty years have also encouraged the expansion of the federal government and the corruption of our culture. The high court has used the interstate commerce clause in the Constitution (Article I, Section 8) to vastly increase the role of the federal government, giving federal agencies the power to control virtually all commerce while giving Congress the authority to ignore its enumerated powers, allowing lawmakers to throw money down any rabbit hole they choose without being held accountable.

The Supreme Court has also contributed to a more coarse and violent American culture. Its decisions to remove prayer and religious values from public schools, along with decisions sanctioning abortion and other behaviors that have proved costly and destructive, are at odds with the values and principles that have always sustained the characteristically decentralized and individualistic American way of life.

## Implications for America's Future

American exceptionalism has steadily declined as more and more Americans have been lured by liberal promises of activist and centralized government, captivated by easy political promises of more benefits and security at no cost. Our economy and culture have been weakened as America has shifted from an individualist to a collectivist society. Perhaps most important, America has drifted deeper and deeper into debt as federal spending and borrowing have increased along with the growing central power in Washington.

Our massive debt is just a symptom of the underlying problems created by our growing and intrusive federal government. America's economic engine that gives us wealth, opportunity, and strength is being smothered by oppressive taxes, litigations, and regulations.

America has gone from being a primary exporter of oil to having a chronic dependency on foreign oil. We are no longer the symbol of financial strength; we are the world's largest debtor. We are not the greatest showcase for free enterprise anymore, as American companies flee to even communist countries to find a better environment in which to do business.

American schools, once the foundation for American character and skills, are now rated among the lowest in the industrialized world. Our roads, bridges, airports, and railroads are deteriorating. Few import and export ships now operate under the American flag because of onerous and costly regulations.

Even those areas of our economy that are still the best in the world are under siege by the federal government. America's health-care system is on a short fuse to join the failing socialized health-care systems in other countries. Now the federal government is attempting to take control of America's telecommunications and Internet industries, led by the most innovative and dynamic companies in the world. All of these negative effects correlate directly with the centralization of power in the federal government.

The big-government precedent that began with presidents Wilson and FDR has never been effectively reduced but has instead been built upon by their White House successors, bringing us to the economic breaking point we face today. More Americans than ever understand today that we can't spend money we don't have. This is a rather recent realization if measured by the behavior of those in Washington for most of the last century and the beginning of the new millennium.

This is a bleak picture, but it is not the end of the story for America. We can turn this around if we act now. The ideas and principles that made America unique and special are still working today. But politicians in Washington who believe they can centrally plan and manage freedom are smothering the very things that have always made America work. Managed freedom is tyranny, pure and simple—and Americans must fight back now or we may never get the chance again.

## The Battle to Save America Has Already Begun

The elections of 2010 marked the beginning of Americans joining the fight to take back their country. Tea Party activists and citizens who attended town halls, rallies, and debates created an awakening unparalleled by any political movement for generations. But conservatives who understand and embrace American exceptionalism remain outnumbered in both houses of Congress, and, unfortunately, the world's best salesman for socialism is still in the White House.

The 2012 elections for the White House and Congress may be the last chance for Americans to turn things around. Americans must be informed and engaged more than ever before. Nearly half of Americans want more from the federal government, which means the 50 percent of Americans who know better have to be smarter and more committed than the other 50 percent who would—and do—trade their freedom for more government promises.

In June 2011, conservatives in the House and the Senate joined with over forty grassroots groups to try to stop Washington's reckless spending and borrowing. President Obama had, for the fourth time in his presidency, asked Congress to increase America's debt limit by another two trillion dollars. The national debt was already at an unsustainable $14.3 trillion, and the President planned to increase the debt by another $10 trillion over the next ten years. Such fiscal irresponsibility is completely indefensible.

At the organizational meeting with members of Congress and the outside groups, I was overwhelmed by the importance of our mission and the increasing difficulty of battling the entrenched political forces in Washington. I recalled Ben Franklin's plea for prayers at the Constitutional Convention in Philadelphia in 1787:

> I have lived, Sir, a long time and the longer I live, the more convincing proofs I see of this truth—that God governs in the affairs of men. And if a sparrow cannot fall to the ground without his notice, is it probable that an empire can rise without his aid? We have been assured, Sir, in the sacred writings that "except the Lord build the house, they labor in vain that build it." I firmly believe this; and I also believe that without his concurring aid we shall succeed in

this political building no better than the Builders of Babel: We shall be divided by our little partial local interests; our projects will be confounded, and we ourselves shall be become a reproach and a bye word down to future age. And what is worse, mankind may hereafter this unfortunate instance, despair of establishing Governments by Human Wisdom, and leave it to chance, war, and conquest.

I therefore beg leave to move—that henceforth prayers imploring the assistance of Heaven, and its blessings on our deliberations, be held in this Assembly every morning before we proceed to business, and that one or more of the Clergy of this City be requested to officiate in that service.

I opened the meeting in prayer and shared a story about a visit I received that day from a lady named Pam. She had driven from Texas to Washington to deliver an urgent message: "Please keep fighting for our country."

Pam believed America was near a total economic and fiscal collapse, and she understood that I—and the few who were willing to stand with me—faced almost impossible odds in our efforts to turn things around. She gave me a key with "FREEDOM" emblazoned on it to keep in my pocket. She also gave me a red ribbon with a silver token that had "1 CHRONICLES 22:13" stamped on one side ("Be strong and courageous. Do not be afraid or discouraged") and COURAGE engraved on the other.

I told the group that day that it was wrong for us to send men and women in our military to fight and die for freedom around the world if we were not willing to fight for freedom here at home.

We did not have to face bullets and bombs, only deceptive politicians and media sources that systemically confuse and mislead our constituents.

Our plan was to get enough Republicans to oppose any increase in the debt limit until the Democrats agreed to three things: (1) cut spending significantly for the upcoming fiscal year, (2) create spending caps that would reduce spending to achieve a balanced budget in the future, and (3) pass a constitutional amendment that would force Congress to maintain a balanced budget after it is ratified by two-thirds of the states.

I was not aware of any Republican who did not agree with our three demands. The only question was: were they willing to stand firm against any increase in the debt limit until President Obama and the Democrats agreed to join us? We knew the President would attempt to frighten Americans about defaulting on our loans and use the media to whip up panic on Wall Street and around the world. The pressure would be enormous to give in and simply let the President borrow more money.

We created the "Cut, Cap, and Balance" pledge—cut spending, cap it, and balance it—to draw a line in the sand so American voters could see which politicians were willing to oppose increasing the debt limit until Congress met our demands. A website was designed to allow members of Congress and candidates to sign up. I hoped thousands of Americans would help give Republicans the courage and resolve to stand firm and hold our ground.

One editorial writer for a major conservative newspaper told me the Cut, Cap, and Balance pledge was a high-risk strategy. I responded that signing the Declaration of Independence was a high-risk strategy as well, and it was time for this generation to pledge our lives, our fortunes, and our sacred honor to save what our Founders gave us.

## Share the Truth

- Misguided political forces have changed America from a republic built on individualism and decentralization to a centralized and more collectivist nation. We must take this country back to a more limited and constitutional government.
- Too many politicians, journalists, and academics have adopted the European secular-socialist policies that have resulted in massive debts and sluggish economies. The economic collapses suffered by Greece and Ireland can happen here, too.
- President Franklin Roosevelt used the Great Depression and World War II to move America toward collectivist programs that expanded dependency on the federal government.
- For most of America's history, the federal government had little or no involvement with public education, health care, transportation, energy, environment, or many of the other functions that have been added despite constitutional limitations. It's time to once again decentralize many of these current federal functions.
- The federal government has an important but limited role in making sure that Americans are safe, that commerce is operating within the rule of law, that there is equality and justice, and that our dollar is sound.
- We must restore constitutional limits and balance the federal government's budget before it's too late. This is not a mere choice but a crucial imperative.

# 4

# No Compromise
# with Democrats

# Introduction by Representative Steve King

America needs to get back on track. The only way to do this is through the private sector. It is the free market that gives entrepreneurs and small businesses an environment where they can thrive, creating jobs and more opportunities for all Americans.

As someone who started and ran his own small business for nearly thirty years, I understand the challenges small businesses face, and as a member of the House Committee on Small Business I have pushed for commonsense policies that will reduce the tax and regulatory burden under which entrepreneurs and business owners must operate. Doing this gives businesses incentive to grow and hire more workers. And it is promoting the entrepreneurial spirit of the American people that will give us real and sustainable economic growth.

Any economic recovery must also include substantial governmental reform. First and foremost, we must balance the federal budget. This will help to restore confidence to financial markets around the world, give banks the confidence to begin lending to small businesses again, and ensure that the next generation of American entrepreneurs isn't saddled with excessive taxes.

We also cannot fix our nation's finances without an honest, grown-up conversation about entitlement reform. Social Security and Medicare are insolvent. This cannot endure.

Our debt and deficit today are at record highs. In 2006, when President Obama was still in the Senate, he said that "increasing America's debt weakens us domestically and internationally," and that *leadership* means not "shifting the burden of bad choices today onto the backs of our children and grandchildren."

I couldn't agree more. So why is the Democratic Party doing exactly that? Why are they "burdening" our children and grandchildren tomorrow by making so many "bad choices" today?

Why is Obama the most antibusiness president in this nation's history? Why is the President's party so opposed to balancing the budget? When Republicans offer solutions to fix entitlements, why do Democrats demonize them, and where are *their* solutions? When conservatives insist that raising the debt ceiling must come with spending cuts, why do liberals want to continue massive spending with no cuts whatsoever?

The Democratic Party simply does not subscribe to the values, traditions, and principles that made America great. In war and politics, the tactic is to attack the enemy's most cherished institutions. Because we hold the values of freedom and the free market dear, they will remain under relentless attack by the Left. We are in an ideological war. Democrats broaden their power base by undermining values and traditions that made America great while continuing to assault Republicans who defend those values and principles. In a time of financial crisis, Democrats see Republicans who insist on fiscal responsibility as the enemy.

It's hard to imagine how a party with such a warped view of reality could offer any real solutions to address the serious economic problems before us. Conservatives must fight hard to elect good or better leaders in the only party that exhibits the will to turn this country around.

There's an old saying: "If you can't beat 'em, join 'em." But if this country is to have a future, joining the Democrats is out of the question.

We must beat them.

One of my best friends in Congress is a Democrat. He is part of a small group of moderate to conservative Democrats in the House known as Blue Dog Democrats. We agree on many things. He believes there should be a constitutional amendment to balance the federal budget. He believes in a strong defense. He is against illegal immigration. He is pro-life. He is a man of genuine faith with a strong commitment to his family.

I once asked him: "You agree with Republicans on almost every issue. So why are you a Democrat?" His answer: "Because I want to help people."

My friend's answer reminds us there are many good people in the Democratic Party who are sincere in their desire to help others. They honestly believe that despite all the evidence to the contrary, the federal government can balance the playing field of life, ensure fairness, improve education, eliminate poverty, and redistribute wealth and prosperity from the haves to the have-nots—all without diminishing the individualist and entrepreneurial character that has always defined America.

Often without knowing it, many Democrats share the big-government philosophy long dominant in Europe, which insists that centralized political power and collectivist solutions will "help people." Many Democrats are not aware that their beliefs are fundamentally opposed to the core principles of American exceptionalism. Their attempts to help people have trapped many Americans in dependency on government, sapped individual responsibility and initiative, and depressed the overall economy. Democratic policies have created more poverty and less opportunity, encouraged depravity, and undermined America's hallmark culture of character and self-reliance.

But to progressives and most Democrats—facts don't seem to matter.

As I expose the dangerous progressive underpinnings of the Democratic Party, I want to remind my readers that there are few Republicans who have been more critical of my own party than me. When I said in 2009 that I would "rather have thirty Republicans" in the U.S. Senate "who believe in the principles of freedom than sixty who believe in nothing at all," it did not sit well with a good number of my GOP colleagues. But it didn't bother me that my comments bothered them. My party needed to hear that it had lost its way. My recent book *The Great American Awakening* chronicles my many battles with party leaders as well as my efforts to elect Republicans who would actually fight for the principles they say they believe in.

Republicans have failed on many counts—each due directly to the party's failure to follow its core principles. Republicans believe in the centrality of the individual in a free society, the dignity of life, constitutionally limited government, low taxes, decentralized political power (federalism and states' rights), equality of opportunity, a strong defense, and a strong culture that reflects America's Judeo-Christian heritage.

Many Republicans in Washington have not been true to the core principles of our party. After gaining the majority in Congress and electing a Republican president in 2000, we violated practically every principle of our party platform. We betrayed the trust of the American people, and in doing so Republicans also betrayed themselves.

But strong grassroots Republican activists, Tea Partiers, and many citizens across the country who weren't even involved in politics initially are now rebuilding the Republican Party around America's founding principles. Many new Republicans—*real* Republicans—were swept into office in the 2010 midterm elections propelled by a groundswell of citizen activism demanding constitutional and limited government.

Countless Americans became united in the 2010 elections in their concern about Washington's out-of-control spending and borrowing, and unsustainable debt. Concerned citizens replaced many Democrats with Republicans in the House and the Senate. Now these same voters vigilantly watch to see if the Republicans they elected keep their promises.

## The Problem with Compromise

The stated goals of the Republican Party reflect the basic tenets of American exceptionalism. Decentralization of political power and a belief in the centrality of the individual in a free society are the principles that should guide Republican policies. While Republican policy makers have often drifted from their moorings, these core principles continue to serve as the GOP's conscience—especially today as Americans wake up to the consequences of a profligate, overbearing central government.

The problems with the Democratic Party are systemic. Their core principles are based on the unreasonable and historically disproven belief that government action is synonymous with success. When Democrats see a problem, they instinctively look to government to solve it. Creating some new government program is always their solution, and whether or not it actually works is never a top concern. Government action and government control are never Democratic last resorts, but the primary goals of their party.

To their credit, Democrats at least believe in their core principles—certainly more than Republicans have in recent years when it comes to fighting for what they believe in.

Democrats see poverty and demand collectivist government action to solve it—not encouragement of character development or increasing the capabilities necessary to help individuals succeed. When Democrats see failing government schools, they never think of allowing competition and more individual choice, but immediately turn to more spending and centralization of government schools.

When President George W. Bush sought to improve public education through No Child Left Behind, he went to Democratic Senator Ted Kennedy to find a compromise. Bush's proposal included more centralized federal control of public education. This frustrated many Republicans. But Bush's plan originally offered an option for states to agree to higher federal standards in return for the flexibility to run their own schools and develop their own education programs. This would encourage states to compete for the best public education systems.

I was opposed to NCLB but believed the opt-out provision would allow some states to demonstrate better ways to improve their schools. But in order to gain Kennedy's and his fellow Democrats' support, Bush was forced to give up the state flexibility provision. Bush had personally promised me that this provision would be in the final plan, but Democrats would have none of it. The Democrats vowed to fight any plan that would reduce federal control of schools.

Bush's compromise with Democrats to pass NCLB resulted in more centralized federal control over public education and, ultimately, more spending to maintain an education system that continues to lose ground and becomes increasingly less competitive with the rest of the world. It should really be called "More Children Left Behind."

Worse, NCLB doubled the size of the already troublesome Department of Education. Ronald Reagan wanted to abolish the Department of Education. He was right.

The same Democratic preference for centralized solutions was on full display when President Bush proposed a plan to help poor seniors pay for prescription drugs. Approximately 25 percent of seniors were without the means to afford their prescribed medication, and Republicans offered several plans to create a safety net to help those in need.

True to form, the Democrats would have none of this. They

demanded a new Medicare prescription plan that provided universal coverage. Every senior citizen, rich or poor, had to have access to the government plan. Their plan was much more costly than Republican plans and drove millions more Americans into dependency on the federal government. Universal coverage was the only plan Democrats would support, so Bush compromised with the Democrats and moved America closer to what was essentially a socialized health-care system.

Virtually every time Republicans compromise with Democrats, we end up with more spending and federal control. Democrats are patient and persistent. Even with a Republican president and a Republican majority in Congress, Democrats were able to force compromises that led to more federal spending and control of education, health care, banking, transportation, and energy. The Democrats were also able to stop almost every Republican attempt to reduce spending, decentralize federal control, and create more choices in education, health care, Social Security, and other government services.

We often hear calls from all quarters for more bipartisanship, cooperation, and compromise. Americans want their elected officials to work together for the good of the country. This sounds entirely reasonable.

So why doesn't it work in Washington?

I believe in compromise and cooperation. As a community leader and professional team builder, I learned the importance of people working together to accomplish shared goals. But that is precisely the problem in Washington: Democrats and Republicans have very few shared goals.

Democrats and Republicans can agree that Americans should

help the poor. But Democrats will not accept any solution that is not a federal government solution. They are much more interested in federal control than successful outcomes. Recent debates over the debt and spending in Congress have revealed two mostly irreconcilable worldviews—that of the Democrats who will always rely on big, activist, and expensive government, and of the party that believes government is too big, too activist, and certainly too expensive. The only compromises Democrats accept are those that increase federal control and spending. Republicans have too often accepted these Democrat "compromises"—which always mean growing the federal government and increasing spending and debt.

That's how we got $15 trillion in debt.

When I served as a leader in my church, the United Way, and the local Chamber of Commerce, I worked with people who had a wide range of ideas about how to accomplish the mission and vision of these organizations. We often compromised about strategies and tactics, and we worked together as teams with no concern for personal biases or who supported which political party. We all shared similar goals, and that allowed us to cooperate for the good of the organization and the people we served.

The same was true in my professional life before politics. I was a strategic planner, team builder, and quality trainer for many organizations. I helped managers and workers learn to respect different abilities and personalities, and I assisted companies in developing a consensus for their mission and vision statements. Once people agreed on their basic goals, they could constructively debate, cooperate, and compromise on how to achieve their objectives and goals.

This is how genuine compromise is supposed to work.

"Compromise" with Democrats has always proved to be an entirely different animal, and a dangerous one at that. While the Democratic Party's stated goals may be to help people, their means to that end is *always* more central control by the federal government. I've come to believe, after spending many years in Washington, that more federal control is some Democrats' actual end—and they simply use the excuse of helping the poor as a means toward that end. Regardless, the Democrats will always believe that the only way to help people is for the government to control all decision making and to spend even more taxpayer dollars.

Republicans and Democrats both want to help the poor, improve education, and make health care available to everyone. But Democrats see government programs instead of individuals. And despite an abundance of evidence that central planning hurts people more than it helps them, Democrats continue to believe that their failures are the result of too little central control and spending.

Telling Republicans to compromise with Democrats is like a coach telling his players to compromise with the players on the opposing team. Can you imagine a coach inspiring his players to work with those other guys, find areas of agreement, and cooperate and compromise? No! The other team is fighting toward a different goal. They are the opposition. Their goals are opposed to your very goals. They are there for one reason—to defeat you. There is no win-win in this sort of situation.

Democrats exist to beat Republicans. Period. They are opposed to our goals of decentralizing political power and encouraging individual freedom. Republicans simply cannot cooperate and compromise with Democrats—we must beat them at the ballot box. Failure to do so will only allow the Democrats to continue destroying this country.

## The Power and Money behind the Democratic Party

Founded in the early nineteenth century, the Democratic Party is the oldest political party in America. Democrats have historically been a center-Left political party but have trended toward the hard Left significantly in recent decades.

Franklin D. Roosevelt was at the presidential helm when the Democratic Party took its first sharp left turn. FDR's attempt to take control of the Supreme Court by stacking it with liberal judges failed, but his New Deal would expand federal government pension programs, empower union bosses, and create new welfare programs for the poor. These programs—always in the name of "helping" the poor and others—planted the seeds that would eventually blossom into the massive dependency and unsustainable debt that characterizes our government today.

Democratic president Lyndon Johnson's Great Society—one of the most misnamed federal programs in this nation's history—accelerated government growth and dependency with a large-scale expansion of welfare and the creation of Medicare. President Jimmy Carter helped establish the Department of Education and began the consolidation of federal control of America's public school system. In this Democratic tradition, President Obama has now effectively nationalized America's health-care and financial systems.

As Democrats have centralized federal control of most

everything—education, health care, banking, housing, communications, energy, transportation, retirement pensions, and many aspects of employment and commerce—they have also consolidated numerous political constituencies who benefit from federal power.

The passage of the Civil Rights Act in the early 1960s consolidated African-American support for the Democratic Party. Republicans have been blamed for segregation and discrimination, even though the segregated South was solidly Democratic. Southern Democrats in Congress were violently opposed to Civil Rights legislation, and it passed only because more than 80 percent of Republicans in the House and Senate also voted for it. Nevertheless, most African-Americans have been convinced that Republicans are opposed to their interests. Today, over 90 percent of black voters regularly support Democratic candidates.

Continued African-American support for Democrats is based on the misperception that Republicans, who now control the South, were largely responsible for Southern segregation policies. Republican opposition to welfare and affirmative action has reinforced the view among African-Americans that Republicans do not support equality or are opposed to minority interests. Few Americans are aware that the Republican Party was founded to abolish slavery, that Abraham Lincoln was the first Republican president, and that Republicans continue to fight for family values and policies, such as school choice, that would largely benefit poor and minority students.

Democratic policies have done far more harm than good for African-Americans. Before President Johnson's welfare expansion, the unwed-birth rate for African-Americans was less than 10 percent. Today, with welfare incentives encouraging out-of-wedlock births, over 70 percent of African-Americans are born out of wedlock. Democrats so often say we need government solutions to solve our problems when what they ultimately do is subsidize those problems. Unwed births are a primary contributor to poverty, high school dropouts, unemployment, drug use, crime, and incarceration, and welfare has seriously harmed the family structure of American families—yet Democrats remain wholly resistant to any reforms. Their answer to how we might finally fix these problems? More spending, more federal control, and, as always, more government.

As I've noted, whether or not federal programs are actually successful does not seem to faze Democrats. The facts or results simply don't matter. The Democrats' goal is more federal control and dependency—and that end in and of itself makes welfare programs a success. A dependent voter is a dependable vote for the Democrats—and unfortunately too many people have become trapped in this cycle of dependency.

Democrats have also endeared themselves to labor unions. They shamelessly pander to union bosses by consistently adding provisions that promote unionization in many unrelated pieces of legislation. President Obama's near-trillion-dollar economic stimulus plan favored construction contracts with unionized employers. Virtually all transportation bills include provisions that favor unionized contractors.

While union membership has dropped precipitously in the private sector to below 10 percent, Democrats have promoted unionization of government workers at every level. Today more than half of all union members work for the government. This has contributed to exorbitant salaries and benefit packages that are bankrupting many states. But this is not a problem for Democrats precisely because union bosses and workers are always dependable votes for Democratic candidates.

Federal and state laws crafted by Democrats force employers and governments to automatically draft union dues from paychecks. In the twenty-eight "forced union" states, workers don't have a choice whether to join organized labor. In these states, if a workplace is unionized, workers are forced to join. Union dues are drafted from their paychecks whether they like it or not (and many most certainly do not). Union dues are then used to make political contributions, over 90 percent of which go to members of the Democratic Party. Democrats are dependent on the dues-based political contributions of unions and the get-out-the-vote pressure on union workers to vote for Democrats. Unions are likewise dependent on Democrats who use government to forcefully expand union membership of private and government employers. Once again—dependent voters always make dependable votes for Democrats.

The Democratic Party has cobbled together other groups who benefit from federal power. Trial lawyers are among the largest financial contributors to the Democratic Party. They are dependent on Democrats to maintain laws that make America the most litigious society in the world. Frivolous lawsuits against employers are out of control and contribute to America's unfriendly business environment. Thousands of American jobs are lost every year as companies move overseas to avoid spending millions of dollars to defend themselves against frivolous lawsuits. Over 90 percent of political contributions from trial lawyers go to Democrats.

Do you see a pattern here?

The largest block of voters for Democrats comes from those who are directly dependent on federal and state governments for their income, health care, housing, and food. This group includes government workers, who make up about 20 percent of the total workforce, and welfare recipients who receive their income, Medicaid, food stamps, free school lunches, and housing subsidies from the government. These dependents pay little or no federal income taxes, making them very susceptible to the standard Democratic "tax the rich" propaganda. Not surprisingly, they too are always dependable votes for the Democratic Party.

Millions of illegal immigrants are now discovering America's free education, health-care, and welfare programs. If Democrats succeed in their goal of making aliens citizens and voters, these illegal immigrants will no doubt quickly become Democratic voters.

An increasing number of government dependents are senior citizens whose primary income is Social Security and who rely heavily on Medicare for their health care. This group includes many middle- and upper-income Americans who have no choice in the matter, in that they are almost forced to become more dependent on government. Medicare is the only health plan available to most seniors. And if they decide not to sign up for Medicare, they lose their Social Security. They are trapped—and because of media bias and shameful and misleading campaign advertising, many seniors simply believe Democrats will protect these programs better than Republicans.

But the fact is that Democrats have allowed Social Security

and Medicare to go bankrupt while lambasting any and all Republican attempts to save these programs. Republicans have only sought to save Social Security and Medicare from insolvency. The Democrats continue to pretend that we have plenty of money and that these programs will never be insolvent.

Republicans say we must face hard realities. Democrats say we must ignore reality.

The Democratic Party derives much of its power from voters and financial supporters who are dependent on centralized government control. The Left favors collectivist programs that keep people trapped in dependency as a matter of ideology and maintaining political control. This is why Democrats must continue to grow government, promise more government "investments," create more government programs, and resist all Republican attempts to limit the growth of federal spending with a balanced budget amendment to the Constitution.

Democrats cannot and will not support a balanced budget amendment to the Constitution that forces Congress to limit spending. This would destroy their entire political platform. To balance the budget would mean Democratic campaigns could no longer be based on promises of more government solutions precisely because those solutions would require increased spending—something a truly balanced budget would forbid. By the very nature of their party, Democrats *have* to increase spending, even if it means bankrupting America. And it is no surprise that recent attempts to introduce a balanced budget amendment have been met with Democratic complaints about balancing the budget on the "backs of the poor."

It's always the same old big-government song with the other

party, and this is why Republicans simply cannot compromise with Democrats. We must beat them.

## Dependency Threatens the Republican Party

The Republican Party elected its first president, Abraham Lincoln, on an abolitionist platform in 1860. It has historically been a center-Right party. Since the Democratic Party's sharp left turn under FDR and his New Deal, Republicans have countered the dominant trend toward collectivism with policies that promote individual responsibility, free enterprise, and states' rights.

After decades of Democratic control, Republicans took the majority in Congress in 1994 with a platform of serious reform. They quickly reformed welfare to increase work requirements and encourage individual responsibility, and they gave states incentives to get welfare recipients real jobs. Republicans, with the help of a strong economy, even balanced the federal budget for a few years (if you don't count the billions of dollars the government was "borrowing" from the Social Security Trust Fund). President Bill Clinton saw the popularity of the Republicans and their platform in 1994 and declared the era of "big government" to be over. But even Clinton probably knew that big government was just getting started.

When George W. Bush won the White House in 2000, Republicans lost their way. Spending and debt increased significantly, and thousands of pork-barrel parochial earmarks were added to every spending bill. Bush compromised with Democrats to expand federal control and spending for education and health care.

In short, Republicans weren't acting like Republicans.

In 2006, many Americans became alarmed at the federal government's out-of-control spending and public opinion soured over war efforts in Iraq. In turn, voters vanquished the Republican majority from Congress. In 2008 Democrats strengthened their majorities and elected Democrat Barack Obama president.

After four years of a Democratic majority and two years of Obama as President, a surge of grassroots activism, led by thousands of Tea Party groups, rallied against exponential increases in government spending, mounting federal debt, and the administration's government takeover of health care. In 2010, citizen activism restored a Republican majority in the House and added six Republicans to the Senate.

Shaking off the big-government Bush years, and faced with an even worse big-government president in Barack Obama, Republicans started acting like Republicans again.

Today, the GOP faces a daunting challenge. With over 50 percent of Americans receiving their income directly or indirectly from a government source, it will be hard to find a majority of Americans who truly desire less government. The Democratic Party has worked long and hard to make this so. Today, dependency on government continues to increase dramatically, and America is near a tipping point—where more voters are receiving benefits from government than paying taxes. This is not only unsustainable financially but politically.

The political support base for the Republican Party is more fragmented and less party-loyal than it is for the Democrats. While Democrats often accuse Republicans of being in the pockets of big business and Wall Street bankers, both groups regularly give more campaign contributions to Democrats than to the GOP. Despite what you may have heard, the "rich people" at Goldman Sachs gave much more in political contributions to Democrats in 2008 than any Republican effort.

You may think the U.S. Chamber of Commerce would be a major supporter of Republicans, but they usually balance their political risk by supporting both Democrats and Republicans. Other conservative organizations such as the National Rifle Association and pro-life groups are not loyal to Republicans. They support candidates in both parties who are in line with their positions.

Unfortunately, almost every formal political organization in America today promotes larger, more centralized government. This means most of the organized political power in America is actively working against the principles of free enterprise and individualism that have made this country successful.

Republican support continues to come primarily from freedom-loving individuals, small businesses, and others who understand that our historic principles and values are essential for American freedom to thrive. Republican voters want more freedom, less government, and less taxation. They want the opportunity to succeed, not government security, guaranteed.

Republican supporters will continue to decrease every year as more Americans become dependent on the government. Dependent voters will naturally elect even big-government progressives who will continue to smother economic growth and spend America deeper into debt. The 2012 election may be the last opportunity for Republicans to win enough votes to win the presidency and a majority in Congress, and enact policies that might turn our nation around from the imminent threat of fiscal calamity.

## Another Compromise with Democrats?

In July 2011, after months of asking Congress to increase the legal borrowing limit for the federal government (for the *fourth* time in his presidency, to be exact), President Obama called Republican and Democratic leaders to the White House to make a deal. Prior to the meeting, the President told the nation we needed to make bold cuts in spending.

But what Democrats say often doesn't match what they do. When leaders from both parties arrived at the White House, President Obama announced that tax increases had to be a part of any deal. Upper-income Americans already pay a larger percent of the nation's taxes than any other country in the world. Still, Obama announced that they must go higher. To the Democrats—a party built on class envy and sustained by emotional appeals—this no doubt sounded like a wonderful proposal. To Republicans, the tax hikes proposed by the President sounded like the quickest way to hurt any economic recovery. Republicans knew from history that any tax hikes would do more to reduce jobs than the debt.

This is what the Democrats consider "compromise."

Meanwhile, Treasury Secretary Timothy Geithner was playing the predictable role of Chicken Little, claiming the sky would fall and the United States would default on its loans if the debt limit was not raised by August 2, 2011. Republicans had a difficult choice to make. We could either capitulate (compromise) by increasing the President's borrowing limit on our national credit card, or stand with the thousands of Americans who had already signed our pledge to "cut, cap, and balance."

This was a critical time for the new Republican majority in the House. A few months earlier, Speaker of the House John Boehner had been snookered when he compromised with the Democrats on the 2011 budget. He thought Obama had negotiated in good faith, but once the details of the agreement had been announced (and after the compromise had passed the Congress), real spending cuts proved to be negligible ($38 billion in cuts, an already insignificant amount, was reduced to $252 million dollars—a measly amount compared to a debt approaching $15 trillion). Voters, who had swept House Republicans back into the majority in the midterm election, rightly began to wonder if these politicians had already forgotten why they were elected.

The debt ceiling showdown was a second chance for Republicans to prove their commitment to cut spending and balance the federal budget. As secret negotiations continued with the President, Republicans in the Senate and House decided to go on the offensive. We introduced the Cut, Cap, and Balance bill and began the process of getting enough cosponsors to pass it in the House where Republicans had a majority.

The Cut, Cap, and Balance bill would give the President the increase in the debt limit that he wanted, but this would be under the condition that there would be reasonable cuts in spending in 2012, caps on spending over the next ten years in order to move toward a balanced budget, and the passing of a balanced budget amendment that would allow the states to decide whether to ratify it or not. It was time for the states and the American people to decide if the federal government should be forced to balance its budget. As with most things, this was a decision the Democratic

Party did not—and does not—want the states to make precisely because liberals fear what the result might be.

When Bill Clinton said the era of big government was over in 1994, it was as opportunistic as it was erroneous. In 2012, it will be up to the American people and the Republican Party to finally make this true.

## Share the Truth

- Democrats continue to insist that federal spending and government programs are the best way to help people and encourage economic growth.
- History confirms that the federal government has done more harm than good when it comes to economic growth, decreasing poverty, and increasing employment.
- The facts don't seem to matter to progressives and Democrats, who insist on government solutions even when the outcomes are harmful to the people they want to help.
- Centralized and collectivist policies encourage government dependency and dependent voters who vote for Democrats and their big-government promises.
- The Democratic platform is based on more government spending, programs, and handouts. They have proven themselves incapable of supporting less spending and a balanced budget.
- Almost every large organized political group in America supports Democrats because these groups benefit from more centralized government power and spending.

- Republican support is fragmented and less party-loyal. Their political base consists primarily of freedom-loving individuals, small businesses, and social conservatives.
- When Republicans compromise with Democrats, government grows and spending increases.
- Republicans cannot compromise with Democrats. We must beat them!

# 5

# Cut Wasteful Spending and Regulatory Red Tape

# Introduction by Senator Tom Coburn

Thirty years ago, President Reagan said in his first inaugural address, "In this present crisis government is not the solution to our problem; government is the problem."

Three decades later, many of our political leaders are still offended by this sentiment. Some of the biggest spenders in Washington consider any desire to roll back government or get America's fiscal house in order "extremism." Of course, they now see the same "extremism" in the Tea Party.

However, the philosophy of Reagan and that of today's Tea Party movement is no more radical than what our Founding Fathers believed. In drafting the Constitution, our Founders created a written charter that specifically limited the role of government. They did this for a very simple reason—the Founders understood that only a small and restrained government was fit for a free society. In a genuinely free society that was to remain free, there would be very little government could effectively do to begin with. Our Founding Fathers understood not only that limited government would work and unlimited government would fail—but that the failure to limit it would make us less free.

The great free market economist Milton Friedman once explained the necessity of limiting the power of government:

"There are four ways in which you can spend money. You can spend your own money on yourself. When you do that, why then you really watch out what you're doing, and you try to get the most for your money. Then you can spend your own money on somebody else. For example, I buy a birthday present for someone. Well, then I'm not so careful about the content of the present, but I'm very careful about the cost. Then, I can spend somebody else's money on myself. And if I spend somebody else's money on myself, then I'm sure going to have a good lunch! Finally, I can spend somebody else's money on somebody else. And if I spend somebody else's money on somebody else, I'm not concerned about how much it is, and I'm not concerned about what I get."

Friedman concluded: "And that's government."

Over the past several decades, these simple theories about less government versus more government have been tested time and again, and the result is always the same—excessive spending and regulation always discourages innovation, while limiting government unlocks innovation and job creation.

Less government always encourages more freedom. Less freedom always coincides with more government.

Still, many in Washington want more government. Since 2000 the size of government has doubled and Washington continues to spend like there's no tomorrow. If more spending really was the answer we would be in the midst of the biggest economic boom in the history of the free world. But so-called federal stimulus packages haven't stimulated anything. Instead, we have seen our credit rating downgraded and are still struggling to pull out of a severe recession.

As Senator DeMint argues, we need to seriously rethink the role of the federal government. We must have a government that spends less and does less. And in those specific areas where government has a legitimate role, it needs to do less much more efficiently.

Rethinking the role of government means having a national debate over who got it right: our Founders, or today's big-spending Washington politicians who are always wanting to expand government?

President Obama has been a consistent and effective defender of the view that more government is the answer. He has even argued that America needs a "Sputnik moment" marked by new "investments" in areas like education, research, and clean energy.

The problem is, all of our "Sputnik moments" over the past few decades have created little more than space junk. Politicians always love to launch new programs with great fanfare but never bother to check on whether they are worth the cost or even if they work. Throughout our federal government, duplicative and wasteful spending continues to crowd out private investment, dampens innovation, and leaves us with nothing but staggering debt.

Washington is reluctant to change its ways, but the good news is you are already having an impact. Every step in the right direction we currently see now in Washington—from ending earmarks, shifting the debate from "How much do we spend?" to "How much do we cut?"—has happened because of you. "We the People" are standing up for this country again and demanding the changes necessary to restore our freedoms.

There is no problem before us that can't be solved. By holding Washington accountable and electing leaders who respect our Founders' vision and our Constitution, We the People can reestablish a government that is limited, more efficient—and, perhaps most important, actually works.

In April of 2011, President Obama set an August deadline for Congress to again increase the nation's debt limit by another $2.4 trillion. We were told we needed to borrow even more money to pay our bills and avoid default on an already overwhelming $14.3 trillion national debt. America was borrowing 43 cents for every dollar we spent—$140 billion a month—and we would soon exceed the legal debt limit signed into law by Obama just over a year before. Federal spending had gotten so out of control that everyone was insisting we just had to borrow trillions more simply to pay the interest on the money already borrowed.

President Obama demanded that Congress increase the debt limit without "any strings attached," meaning essentially that he did not want any spending cuts. By late July, Congress could still not reach an agreement with the White House. The nation and the world were in a panic—everyone knew America could not pay its bills without borrowing more money.

The United States has had a AAA credit rating for decades. This superior rating has allowed us to amass huge debts at low interest rates. But even with low interest rates, we are on a course to pay more than $1 trillion in annual interest payments within the next ten years. This is more than we now spend on Social Security or Medicare annually. If the rating agencies downgrade our credit, America might have to pay higher interest rates on both existing and new loans. And for every percent increase in the interest rate on our debt, taxpayers will pay another $1 trillion over the next ten years.

America does not even have the ability to service our current debt at higher interest rates; much less the $10 trillion in new debt Obama has planned over the next decade. And interest rates will certainly go up as all the indebted nations of the world compete for a shrinking pool of credit. Yet the President asked Congress to increase our debt by another $2.4 trillion without any plan to reduce spending.

In July of 2011, the major rating agencies, Standard & Poor's (S&P) and Moody's, warned that if the United States raised its debt limit without a credible, long-term deficit reduction plan, they would downgrade our credit rating. The President's only response was to again insist on raising taxes.

There was a stalemate in Washington.

Republicans in the House responded by passing the Cut, Cap, and Balance bill, which would cut spending in 2012, cap spending over the next ten years, and raise the debt limit by $2.4 trillion—but only with the condition that both houses of Congress pass a balanced budget amendment and send it to the states for ratification. This was the only plan that could possibly avoid a credit downgrade. It was, in fact, the only plan at all—since neither the President nor the Democratic majority in the Senate had produced any plan at all.

Still, Senate Majority Leader Harry Reid called Cut, Cap, and Balance the worst legislation in history, and the President condemned a balanced budget amendment to the Constitution as extreme. Obama arrogantly said, "We don't need a constitutional amendment to do our job." Well, Mr. President, yes, in fact, we do need an amendment. How has Congress "doing its job" of spending taxpayer dollars wisely worked out for America? The truth is, Washington hasn't been doing its job for a very long time.

Hundreds of conservative organizations and Tea Party groups got behind the responsible Cut, Cap, and Balance plan. After the House passed it with a large majority (including five Blue Dog Democrats) Senator Reid promised a full debate in the Senate.

Many polls showed increased public support for the bill and a balanced budget amendment. Over 70 percent of Americans supported a balanced budget amendment to the Constitution, and a CNN poll found 66 percent of Americans supported the Cut, Cap, and Balance bill (though CNN did not report the results of their own poll). The media attempted to ignore the Republican plan, but public support continued to grow.

Despite overwhelming public support, Reid decided to table the Cut, Cap, and Balance bill and avoid a public debate. Every Democratic senator voted to table the bill, even though over twenty of them were actually on record supporting a balanced budget amendment to the Constitution. Reid pronounced the bill dead—but I hoped Americans would prove him wrong.

## Rethinking the Role of the Federal Government

Solving America's economic and fiscal problems means cutting spending and waste at the federal level—but equally important, it means rethinking the role of the federal government. The federal government doesn't need to do more to solve our problems—it should do less, it can do less, and it must do less. Many Democrats consider this sentiment extreme or a threat, but it truly is the new reality. Washington must begin to let go of programs we can't afford and cannot competently manage.

If the federal government simply cuts spending on existing programs, the results could be harmful. Cuts in spending without reducing the bureaucracy and control of the federal government in education, welfare, transportation, energy development, health care, and other important programs will hurt many Americans. Necessary reductions must be in conjunction with a vast reassessment and reassignment of government functions. The quality of these programs will decline and services will deteriorate if spending is cut without significant changes in the role of the federal government. Cuts in spending for Social Security and Medicare without reforms will result in broken promises and benefit cuts to seniors. Americans will have to work beyond when they expected to in order to receive the Social Security benefits they have paid for all their lives. Physicians will be paid less to see Medicare patients, and seniors will not be able to find doctors who accept Medicare. If we do nothing, as Democrats suggest, people will in fact suffer.

Likewise, America's military and defenses will be weakened if we cut defense spending without rethinking our role in the world, eliminating waste, and developing an affordable strategy to defend our nation. As Senator Tom Coburn has pointed out, we would actually have a stronger military if we could reduce the vast inefficiencies and rampant waste that have come to define Pentagon spending.

We also cannot afford to continue being the world's policeman or sugar daddy. Senator Rand Paul has pointed out that there are two extremes in foreign policy—being everywhere all the time, or being nowhere none of the time. Currently, the United States is far closer to the first extreme of trying to do too much in too many places. Of course, America must have the ability to defend our nation and our interests around the world, but because of irresponsible political management of the nation's fiscal condition, we simply can no longer afford to intervene in every crisis around the world. The practical limits to what government can accomplish or afford at home also applies abroad—and perhaps fiscal sanity will also lead to a wiser foreign policy.

## Reducing Waste, Fraud, and Duplication

As we have the necessary debate over how to downsize many federal programs and devolve their functions back to the states, there are many easy targets to reduce spending without compromising the quality of government services.

Fortunately, pork-barrel earmarks such as the infamous "bridge to nowhere" have been banned, at least for now. But wasteful Washington spending still unnecessarily consumes trillions of taxpayer dollars. We will never get our nation's spending and the debt under control until we reduce the waste, fraud, and duplication in every area of the federal government.

In February of 2011, Senator Tom Coburn released a report from the General Accounting Office (GAO), a watchdog federal agency that assesses the effectiveness and efficiency of federal programs. The report exposed widespread waste and duplication in federal spending.

"This report confirms what most Americans assume about their government. We are spending trillions of dollars every year and nobody knows what we are doing. The executive branch doesn't know. The congressional branch doesn't know. Nobody knows," Senator Coburn said.

Coburn added, "This report also shows we could save taxpayers hundreds of billions of dollars every year without cutting services. And, in many cases, smart consolidations will improve service. GAO has identified a mother lode of government waste and duplication that should keep Congress busy for the rest of the year."

Here are just a few of the GAO findings and examples of duplication, mismanagement, and waste in the federal budget, as exposed by Coburn's report:

- *Dangerous lack of coordination regarding defenses against biological terror threats.* At least five departments, eight agencies, and more than two dozen presidential appointees oversee $6.48 billion related to bioterrorism. GAO writes: "There is no national plan to coordinate federal, state, and local efforts following a bio-terror attack, and the United States lacks the technical and operational capabilities required for an adequate response."
- *$1 trillion for special tax benefits, many of which are redundant.* GAO writes: "For fiscal year 2009, the U.S. Department of

the Treasury listed a total of 173 tax expenditures, some of which were the same magnitude or larger than related federal spending for some mission areas."

- *Financial literacy education offered by a government with a $14 trillion debt.* Twenty agencies operate fifty-six programs dedicated to financial literacy, but GAO and agencies can't estimate what they cost (not exactly good models for responsible financial management).

- *Economic development programs with little evidence of economic development.* The federal government runs eighty economic development programs across four agencies at a cost of $6.5 billion.

- *Highways programs have not been rebooted since 1956.* The Department of Transportation (DOT) spends $58 billion on one hundred separate programs run by six thousand employees from among five DOT agencies. GAO says the programs have "not evolved to reflect current priorities in transportation planning."

- *Senseless duplication among military branches.* GAO found that the military wastes untold billions on duplication and overlap. For instance, Army and Air Force transportable base equipment, which includes mobile housing and dining facilities, could be used by both branches of service, but are not.

Senator Coburn—a perennial warrior against waste and duplication in the federal government—released another report in April 2011 titled: "The National Science Foundation: Under the Microscope." NSF spends $6.9 billion annually and is our nation's premier broad-based scientific research agency. NSF is the major source of federal backing in mathematics and computer sciences, and it spends billions more in important fields such as engineering, biology, physics, and technology. But Coburn found that while the NSF has an important mission and contributes to meaningful scientific discovery, there are pervasive problems at the agency:

- NSF lacks adequate oversight of its grant funding, which has led to mismanagement, fraud, and abuse and lack of knowledge regarding research outcomes.
- NSF is prone to extensive duplication within the agency and across the federal government.
- NSF wastes millions of dollars on low-priority projects.

The National Science Foundation wastes millions of dollars on many questionable projects. Among the grants that have been funded by the NSF are:

- a study suggesting that playing the game FarmVille on Facebook helps adults develop and maintain relationships
- an analysis of how quickly parents respond to trendy baby names
- a grant to produce songs about science, including a rap called "Money 4 Drugz" and a misleading song titled "Biogas is a Gas, Gas, Gas"
- a study on why the same teams always seem to be dominating March Madness
- millions of dollars to figure out that people who often post pictures on the Internet from the same location at the same time are usually friends

- a study on whether online dating site users are racist in their dating habits

Coburn concluded that NSF lacks adequate oversight of its grant funding, which has led to significant mismanagement, fraud, and abuse. Internal reports and audits reveal systemic problems with the agency's grant administration, financial controls, and overall stewardship of scientific research dollars. The report also reveals that mismanagement has led to hundreds of millions of dollars lost to ineffective contracting. Among the fraudulent and inappropriate expenditures highlighted in this report:

- 47 joint trips to the tune of $144,152 for a pair of romantically involved NSF employees
- bowling and amusement park trips using research funds
- pervasive Internet-porn surfing by NSF employees
- millions spent on alcohol and unrelated costs

Coburn discovered numerous duplications of NSF's services, both within the agency and across the federal government. NSF is one of at least 15 federal departments, 72 subagencies, and 12 independent agencies engaged in federal research and development. An NSF-led analysis of the federal research budget explains that the federal government has "17 science agencies that manage 17 different data silos, with different identifiers, different reporting structures, and different sets of metrics." Taxpayers often pay for duplicative research and no one notices.

The GAO report that Senator Coburn ordered proves beyond any doubt that wasteful, ineffective, and duplicative programs exist in every department of the federal government. NSF is just one of hundreds of programs that are wasting tax dollars for no reason due to no oversight. Some of those programs listed under "General Mismanagement" in the report include:

- *Unneeded and unused property.* The federal government currently owns 55,557 buildings with a collective value of $96 billion that are either underutilized or not utilized at all. Taxpayers must pick up the cost to maintain these properties, most of which serve little or no purpose. In addition to the millions of dollars in unnecessary maintenance costs that could be saved, billions of dollars in revenues could be generated simply by selling off these unnecessary holdings.

- *Wasteful printing and publication.* Thousands of copies of the *Congressional Record* are printed every day. Every member of the Senate receives numerous copies every morning, many of which are never opened or read. It will cost more than $28 million this year to publish the *Congressional Record*, even though it is publicly available online. Congress spends more than $4 million on other publications every year, such as the House and Senate journals. These represent just a fraction of the cost of the many and various publications printed by the federal government that could be reduced by limiting the number of copies produced. In addition to mass-produced government publications, civilian federal employees spend about $440 million for printing considered to be unnecessary—which amounts to more than $1 million a day.

- *Bogus bonuses for failed contractors.* Every year, federal agencies award billions of dollars of bonuses, or award fees, to federal contractors for projects that go over budget or fail to meet basic performance requirements. Between 1999 and 2004, the Department of Defense alone paid $8 billion in unwarranted bonuses to contractors for programs with severe cost overruns, performance problems, and delays. Likewise, the Centers for Medicare and Medicaid Services pays more than $312 million per year in bonuses to nursing homes that provide below-average care and have many past violations of health and safety regulations. Prohibiting the payment of bonuses and award fees to contractors for shoddy work—which any efficient government would never allow in the first place—could save billions of dollars every year.

- *Unpaid taxes owed by federal employees.* Federal employees have failed to pay $3 billion in federal taxes. This includes nearly $2.5 million owed by employees of the U.S. Senate. It is simply common sense that we require federal employees to act responsibly with their taxpayer-funded salaries and comply with the law by fully paying their taxes. Anything less is an insult to the hardworking American people who fund the government.

These are just a few of the thousands of examples of programs that waste billions of dollars of taxpayer money every year. The amount of waste is as unnecessary as it is staggering. You might think the President and Congress would jump at the opportunity to use an example like the GAO report to save billions in federal spending and to make federal services more efficient. Not a chance—and in fact they often attack conservatives as being extreme for even bringing it up.

Needless to say, there has been little effort in Washington to address the waste, fraud, and duplication, even though politicians have known about these problems for years. The reason: it is always unpopular to cut a program and usually very popular to create a new one—with even more spending. Every government program—no matter how wasteful or ineffective—has constituents who benefit from it and who will howl in protest at the mere suggestion of cuts or reforms.

With the nation drowning in debt, it is imperative that we elect a new class of responsible political leaders who will wage a full-scale assault on wasteful Washington spending. And since the President controls the executive branch, with tens of thousands of bureaucrats who in turn control these ineffective programs, we need a new president who will finally exert real leadership to reorganize and streamline wasteful federal agencies.

## Cutting Regulations That Crush Our Economy

America is literally on the verge of an economic catastrophe—yet Washington politicians are unwilling to address glaringly obvious waste and duplication. If our current policies continue, severe economic disruptions may occur even before the 2012 elections.

Democrats claim that cutting spending will hurt the poor, disadvantaged, and elderly—but not cutting spending will hurt each of these groups and then some. Liberals insist that less government spending will hurt the economy—even as a government far too large continues to hurt the economy. Reforming and streamlining federal services will deliver more cost-efficient and effective services to the people who need them. Less government spending will leave more money in the private sector to create jobs, thus further helping the very constituencies Democrats claim Republicans want to harm.

Our future is certainly in jeopardy if we don't make some hard choices now, but spending cuts and reforms of federal programs need not be a doomsday scenario. All Americans face the current crisis posed by an unsustainable government, and all Americans will be better off if we reduce the size and scope of the federal government and restore a constitutionally limited government.

In addition to cutting obviously wasteful and duplicative programs, Washington must eliminate job-killing regulations that are smothering America's free enterprise economic system. An analysis of the current regulatory environment issued by the Heritage Foundation on July 25, 2011, concluded:

> Following a record year of rulemaking, the Obama administration is continuing to unleash more costly red tape. In the first six months of the 2011 fiscal year (FY), 15 major regulations were issued, with annual costs exceeding $5.8 billion and one-time implementation costs approaching $6.5 billion. No major rulemaking actions were taken to reduce regulatory burdens during this period. Overall, the Obama administration imposed 75 new major regulations from January 2009 to mid-FY 2011, with annual costs of $38 billion. There were only six major deregulatory

actions during that time, with reported savings of just $1.5 billion.

This flood of red tape will undoubtedly persist, as hundreds of new regulations stemming from the vast Dodd-Frank financial regulation law, Obamacare, and the EPA's global warming crusade advance through the regulatory pipeline—all of which further weakens an anemic economy and job creation, while undermining Americans' fundamental freedoms. Action by Congress as well as the President to stem this regulatory surge is essential.[1]

The regulatory stranglehold on America's economy impacts every business and every job. Testifying at a House hearing on July 14, 2011, Karen R. Harned, the executive director of the National Federation of Independent Business, told Congress: "A recent study by Nicole and Mark Crain for the U.S. Small Business Administration Office of Advocacy found that the total cost of regulation on the American economy is $1.75 trillion per year... The study found that for 2008, *small businesses spent $10,585 per employee on regulation,* which amounts to 36 percent more per employee than their larger counterparts." (Emphasis added.)

Small businesses create the majority of new jobs in America, so the regulatory burden placed on them from Washington politicians and bureaucrats significantly impacts unemployment and hurts the economy. Still, the steady stream of regulations just keep coming from the Obama administration. Testifying at the same House hearing, W. Kirk Liddell, president & CEO of IREX Corporation, reported, "One study by the Manufacturers Alliance/MAPI estimates that the most stringent ozone proposal being considered *would* *result in the loss of 7.3 million jobs by 2020 and add $1 trillion in new regulatory costs per year between 2020 and 2030.*" (Emphasis added.)

The Obama administration appears to be going after every industry, even farmers. Kevin Rogers, president of the Arizona Farm Bureau Federation and a fourth-generation farmer, also testified at the July 14 house hearing, "It is no exaggeration to say that the onslaught of federal regulations now confronting farmers and ranchers across America is truly overwhelming." Testifying about proposed new regulations for farmers, Rogers reported, "The EPA estimates over 37,000 agricultural facilities will be covered, at an average cost of more than $23,200 per permit, *resulting in costs of over $866 million to producers.*" (Emphasis added.)

The EPA is one of the best examples of the absurd and out-of-control regulatory environment in Washington. The EPA even recently decided that since milk contains oil, it has the authority to force farmers to comply with new regulations to file "emergency management" plans to show how they will cope with spilled milk. This is not a joke. The EPA literally demands to know how farmers will train "first responders" and build "containment facilities" if there is a flood of spilled milk.

Commenting on this ridiculous EPA rule in *National Review*, Thomas Sowell wrote:

> Since there is no free lunch, all of this is going to cost the farmers both money and time that could be going into farming—and is likely to end up costing consumers higher prices for farm products.
>
> It is going to cost the taxpayers money as well, since the EPA is going to have to hire people to inspect farms,

inspect farmers' reports, and prosecute farmers who don't jump through all the right hoops in the right order. All of this will be "creating jobs," even if the tax money removed from the private sector correspondingly reduces the jobs that can be created there.[2]

Public outrage over the EPA's "Spilled Milk Regulation" eventually shamed the agency into repealing the ruling, but there is plenty of room for more outrage—and shaming. In the first six months of 2011, 364 new rules totaling 46,184 pages of regulations had been proposed or enacted by the Obama administration. The only regulation repealed was the "Spilled Milk Regulation."

State and local governments are taking their cues from the federal government (often by force) and adding onerous regulations. Things have become so ridiculous that in some states, children's lemonade stands have been shut down and the parents fined up to $500. I wish I was kidding. Mark Johanson, writing in *International Business Times* on August 2, 2011, reported:

In the month of July alone, at least five makeshift lemonade stands were shut down. In some cases, the "offenders" were charged up to $500. Lemonade stands, which were once a great way to teach kids how to actually make money for themselves, now serve as a harsh lesson in governmental control. Let's take a look at each case on a state-by-state basis:

- *In Wisconsin: Appleton police sorry for lemonade stand shutdown.* Ten-year-old Lydia Coenen and her 9-year-old sister Vivian Coenen were near their Appleton home Sunday morning, preparing to sell lemonade to people heading to a car show. But an officer told them the sales were prohibited by city ordinance. The law went into effect last month and bars licensed vendors from selling food and drinks within a two-block radius of a special event.

- *In Georgia: Police in Midway, Ga. Order Lemonade Stand Closed.* Three Midway girls wanted to pay for a trip to a water park. They needed money, so they set about making it. They were going to make it the old fashioned way. They wanted to earn it. However, they didn't get a business license, a peddler's permit, or a food permit. That is a $50 per day cost, or $180 per year according to Fox-5 in Atlanta that reported this vigilance of local police officers.

- *In Maryland: Kids' Lemonade Stand Shut Down; Parents Fined $500.* You can make a fortune selling parking spots outside the US Open, but don't even dream of setting up a lemonade stand. A county inspector ordered the Marriott and Augustine kids to shut down the stand they set up on Persimmon Tree Rd, right next to Congressional. And after they allegedly ignored a couple of warnings, the inspector fined their parents $500.

- *In Iowa: Girl's lemonade stand shut down.* Police closed down a lemonade stand in Coralville last week, telling its 4-year-old operator and her dad that she didn't have a permit. An officer told Abigail Krutsinger's father Friday that she couldn't run the stand as RAGBRAI bicyclers poured into Coralville. A city ordinance says food vendors must apply for a permit and get a health inspection. Abigail's dad, Dustin Krutsinger, said the ordinance and its enforcers are going too far if they force a 4-year-old to abandon her lemonade stand.

- *In Texas: Lemonade stand shut down by officers in Texas.* A 12-year-old girl and her little brother were just trying to earn a few dollars for their two hermit crabs when a city code enforcement officer in Texas came and shut them down. The officer told their grandmother that the children needed a permit to sell lemonade, and their grandmother was ticketed for the offense. "I was mad," the 12-year-old said. "I don't understand why someone would want to do that to two kids and their grandma."[3]

Lamenting the demise of lemonade stands, Linton Weeks of National Public Radio writes: "There is no catchier, kitschier symbol of the American spirit than a lemonade stand. It represents not only a way of life, but a way of making a living. It is capitalism and leisure, refreshment and resourcefulness, enterprise and summer skies all squeezed together—stirred in with lemons and sugar and water—and sold by the glass for whatever the market will bear."

## Solutions to Waste and Regulations

Every dollar spent by the federal government is a dollar spent less effectively. Every dollar spent in the private sector is a dollar spent more effectively. Of course, there are essential functions of government such as defense that require tax revenue. Even so, those essential functions are few and limited, as outlined in our Constitution. Taxes and limited government expenditures are necessary, but wasteful Washington spending is out of control, and regulatory overreach by Washington bureaucrats is destroying our economy.

Trillions of dollars are now being wasted by Washington, and trillions more are being lost by an economy burdened by regulations and regulatory uncertainty. Millions of jobs have been lost and hundreds of American businesses have moved operations to other countries to avoid high taxes, absurd regulations, and costly litigation.

Why are we doing this to ourselves? Even in the face of economic recession, high unemployment, unsustainable debt, a weakening dollar, and credit downgrades, President Obama demands even more spending and churns out new regulations. Such illogical thinking can be understood only in the context of Washington's addiction to spending and the Democratic Party's commitment to centralized political power and collectivism.

We can begin to change this only by voting President Obama out of office and making sure the Democrats lose majority power in the U.S. Senate. I just hope our country can survive until the 2012 elections.

History tells us that a Republican victory alone will not be enough. Here's what Republicans must do if Americans give them back control of the government in November of 2012.

- *Sunset selected federal agencies, programs, and regulations.* Federal agencies, programs, and regulations should not be eternal. They should be authorized for a limited period of time and reauthorized with congressional approval at predetermined intervals. Agency leaders should regularly have to make a case for the continuation of their programs and regulations. This would eliminate wasteful and duplicative programs, and force agencies to eliminate costly and unnecessary regulations.

- *Utilize the 1996 Congressional Review Act.* Congress has the authority to veto any rule or regulation created by the executive branch. Congress has failed to exercise their authority because of Democrats' resistance. This authority has been used successfully only one time. It's time to start using it again and more often.

- *Adopt the REINS Act.* This proposal, offered by Senator Rand Paul, would require congressional approval of any rule or regulation that has more than a $100 million impact on the economy. If enacted, it would significantly slow the current pace of job-killing regulations.

- *Repeal ObamaCare and Dodd-Frank financial reform.* These two laws alone will cost the American economy trillions of dollars and millions of jobs. ObamaCare will result in government control of America's health-care system, cost taxpayers trillions, and destroy the best health-care system in the world. The Dodd-Frank law gives the federal government control over credit, banks, and the financial markets. By controlling America's financial system, this law will restrict economic growth and give the federal government effective control over our entire economy. Our government has already proved it cannot be trusted with the economic power it has now. To give it even more is lunacy.

- *Congress must do its job.* Congress is responsible for the oversight of federal agencies. Dozens of committees in the House and Senate are charged with keeping agencies accountable and effective. Congress must do its job. Every year, each committee of Congress should present recommendations for the elimination of government programs and regulations. They should hold public hearings to expose waste and costly regulations, and pass legislation to eliminate or consolidate agencies, programs, and regulations.

## Share the Truth

- Wasteful Washington spending, fraud, and duplication unnecessarily cost taxpayers and the economy trillions of dollars.
- Burdensome government regulations are smothering America's economy and killing millions of jobs.
- America's budget deficits and national debt could be reduced substantially without reducing government services simply by eliminating waste and needless regulations.
- These commonsense changes will not happen until President Obama is defeated and the Democratic majority in the Senate is replaced with conservatives.

# 6

# Freedom Solutions
# That Work

# Introduction by Political Pundit Jack Hunter

As a columnist and talk-radio personality, I've conversed with countless fellow conservatives over the years, and a general breakdown of what most would like to see is as follows: the size and scope of Washington, D.C., drastically diminished; the decentralization of power back to the states; a serious reassessment of our current unsustainable policies; less degradation of traditional American culture; a freer market with fewer regulations and obstacles for business; strong values; secure borders; and an earnest return to the U.S. Constitution.

This is basic American conservatism 101, and it should really come as no surprise that most conservatives would like to see a more conservative government. But why haven't we? I've been a conservative for my entire adult life and for all of that time government has gotten bigger. This has been especially true when Republicans have been in power.

What went wrong?

There was a time in this country when conservatism was defined primarily by intellectuals, writers, and various thinkers who promoted certain principles that politicians could either accept or reject. Influential thinkers like Russell Kirk, Friedrich Hayek, Richard Weaver, Ludwig von Mises, William F.

Buckley, and various others gave shape to a distinctly American philosophy of limited government, which statesmen like Senator Barry Goldwater and later Governor Ronald Reagan would embrace and build presidential campaigns on. In those days, being a conservative really meant something specific, and subsequently, during Goldwater's high tide of the early 1960s and before Reagan eventually became president, the term *conservative* was embraced by only a small minority of politicians. Back then, calling oneself a conservative meant taking a real stand, often incurring backlash and negative political consequences. Just ask Barry Goldwater.

Today, virtually every Republican politician calls him- or herself a conservative—thanks mostly to Reagan's triumph and influence. But as the term became more universal, the actual philosophy was diminished. For at least the past two decades, countless so-called conservative Republicans have consistently given us a Democrat-lite agenda, doing almost nothing to slow the march toward big government. The last Republican president was perhaps the worst imposter—a "compassionate conservative" who drastically expanded the Department of Education that Reagan once wanted to abolish, who gave us a massive new entitlement with Medicare Plan D, and who doubled the overall size of government and the national debt.

Of course, "compassionate" conservatism was anything but; it was simply the latest watering down of the real limited government philosophy developed by past brilliant thinkers and once championed on the political front by Goldwater and Reagan. Most Republican politicians had become entirely comfortable with promoting themselves as "conservative" for the purposes of winning elections, but had no real desire to promote substantively conservative agendas. With the arguable exception of the Republican Revolution of 1994 in which the GOP took over the House, denouncing President Bill Clinton's big government policies, for decades the Goldwater-Reagan tradition was absent on the Right in any real sense. Even much of the conservative media, on talk radio, in magazines, and on cable news, steadily confused partisanship with advancing limited-government principles. Promoting conservatism became more advertisement than advisement. And it was this seemingly permanent political rut that compelled so many conservatives to reflexively excuse the big-government excesses of President Bush.

But not every conservative made excuses. Some still valued the principles of limited government and stuck to their guns. My own senator from South Carolina, Jim DeMint, was one of them.

When the Medicare Plan D debacle was unfolding—the largest entitlement expansion since the administration of Lyndon Johnson—DeMint strongly opposed it. Because of this, DeMint was among the few Republican leaders Bush summoned to the White House for daring to buck the President and his party. Bush told DeMint that he understood he was in a tough race, and the president assured the senator that the administration had an eye on his upcoming election down in South Carolina. Still, DeMint wouldn't budge. Not long after, White House officials began calling GOP operatives around South Carolina to pressure them to support Jim's Republican primary opponent. The *Washington Post*'s Ezra Klein even reported the incident: "The leadership told Rep. Jim DeMint that they would cut off funding for his Senate race in South Carolina if he didn't vote for the bill."

But DeMint never flinched. He knew what the true conservative position was and stuck to it—even when his own party was routinely abandoning every limited-government principle it had ever espoused. As Senator DeMint explained, "During the Bush administration, when Republicans controlled Washington, spending and earmarks exploded.... We expanded federal control of education and health care, increased the national debt exponentially, while making no effort to fix the tax code, save Social Security and Medicare, or reduce the size of the federal government—all Republican platform promises."

DeMint added, "You could accuse Republicans of a lot of things, but you could never convict us of being too conservative!"

But at the end of Bush's term, and as President Obama began to rev up his unprecedented statist agenda, something wonderful happened—conservatives began to look more to leaders like Jim DeMint than to the old, big-government Republican guard. The grassroots began to rediscover the philosophy of Goldwater. They revisited the promise of Reagan.

Finally, conservatives began to wake up.

In the midst of bank bailouts, federal "stimulus," and a worsening economy, the grassroots Right became fed up with a Democratic president hell-bent on destroying business, individual freedom, and the Constitution. Conservatives also became fed up with a Republican Party that had either been ineffective in stopping the Democrats or too busy copying them. April 15, 2009—Tax Day—gave rise to massive and spontaneous gatherings across the country in the form of Tea Party rallies, in which Americans disgusted with the status quo of both parties made their voices heard.

Yesterday's "conservative" Republicans were no longer considered sufficiently conservative by the awakened and empowered grassroots. Thanks to the Tea Party, Rand Paul bucked the GOP establishment to become Kentucky's next junior senator. In Utah, Mike Lee challenged a sitting Republican senator and won. DeMint helped both men in their primaries—and Paul and Lee would later join DeMint in the Senate to become an indomitable trio, the tip of the spear in a new revolution.

It is a cliché to say that before things can get better they must get worse, but President Obama has undoubtedly proven this true—as the notion of our children and grandchildren being saddled with a $15 trillion dollar national debt continues to be too much for most Americans to bear. That this president and his party would commandeer such large parts of the American economy, through health-care legislation and monstrous regulation, or insist on further collectivization of a government already too heavily concentrated—this is the sort of insanity this country cannot and will not endure.

The silver lining to the Democrats' dark cloud is that concerned Americans are more open than ever to precisely the type of solutions real conservatives have long desired: drastic reductions in spending; decentralization of power; reassessment of costly and unnecessary domestic and foreign policies; and perhaps most significant—a return to constitutional government.

As Democrats continue to offer big-government solutions that millions of Americans now loudly reject, Republicans have a grand opportunity to transform public zeal for cutting government into legislation. America must become more energy independent and now is the time. Public education must be devolved and now is the time. We need free market solutions to healthcare costs. Our tax structure must be overhauled and diminished. Spending must be cut. Future spending must be capped. Our budget must be balanced.

The status quo must end.

The new fault line in American politics is between those who want to limit government and those who still consider it unlimited. This line transcends partisanship. My greatest fear is not only that Obama and his party will irreparably wreck this country, but that the Republicans will aid them by eventually reverting to their old big-government form. We can always count on the Democrats to be awful. But can we count on a loyal opposition to substantively oppose them—especially at this increasingly fragile, make-or-break, now-or-never juncture in our history?

For conservative solutions to work, we must always remember what conservatism is as well as what it isn't, and look to principled leaders who can tell the difference.

Jim DeMint is one of those leaders, and the freedom-based solutions he proposes represent an opportunity to build a brighter—and more conservative—American future.

On August 1, 2011, after weeks of endless haggling and posturing between President Obama and Congress, a deal to raise the nation's debt limit was passed and signed into law. The next day the U.S. debt shot up by another $234 billion. The total U.S. debt stood at $14.58 trillion—which exceeded the total size of the American economy for the first time since World War II.

By Washington's standards, this debt deal represented a historic sea change. Instead of talking about how much we could spend and how much pork we could take home to our constituents, we were actually talking about how much we should cut spending.

Unfortunately, it was just that—all talk.

Advocates of the debt deal said it reduced spending and cut deficits. Only in Washington-speak was this true. In the real world, it was a complete lie. The much-touted spending "cuts" were simply reductions in planned spending increases. Only in Washington can an increase in spending be considered a cut—and discretionary spending would *increase* nearly a trillion dollars over the next decade with this plan.

In reality, the so-called deficit reduction plan actually increased the national debt by $1 trillion a year for the next decade. This deal also established a super committee of twelve congressmen and senators who were given the power to raise taxes with only a simple majority of members from both houses of Congress. Conservatives would have little power to stop any large tax increases or bad policies recommended by the committee.

Keep in mind—even this awful agreement, which featured no real cuts or substantive reforms, was represented by the Democrats as the Tea Party taking over. This shows just how threatened the Washington establishment is by even the mere recognition of the fact that spending is an issue.

I was joined by eighteen other conservative Republican senators in voting against the debt deal. We believed it was not only stupid but immoral to continue piling enormous debt onto our children and grandchildren. All forty-seven Republican senators and just about every Republican in the House supported a real debt reduction plan—Cut, Cap, and Balance—which would have put our country on a path toward a balanced budget. But every Democrat in the Senate opposed our plan to balance the budget, and although the House passed it overwhelmingly with minimal Democratic support, Senate Majority Leader Harry Reid tabled the bill and refused to allow any public debate.

Few outside of Washington were impressed with the final deal to supposedly control spending and address the debt. A few days after the passage of the debt deal, the stock market suffered its worst one-day loss since 2008. At the same time, Standard &

Poor's downgraded America's credit rating. We lost our cherished AAA rating for the first time in history. Mind you, the biggest advocates for the bad debt deal had warned that not raising the debt ceiling would be disastrous precisely because the failure to do so might damage America's credit rating.

The struggling U.S. economy, global financial crises, economic decline, Washington's refusal to deal honestly with our exploding debt, and Obama's antibusiness policies—all of these were crushing America's hopes for an economic recovery.

The cumulative impact of more than two years of Obama's policies was working against any hope for an economic recovery. The President and his party had made a bad situation much worse. Americans were fed up and the nation was desperate for real solutions—not simply more political theater like the smoke-and-mirrors debt limit deal.

## Freedom Solutions That Will Work

With America quite literally on the verge of an economic disaster, and almost no hope of changing our course until at least the 2012 elections, it is critical that Republicans propose positive alternatives. Naturally, most Americans don't trust what anyone from Washington says these days—so it is our task to prove that conservatives have the right solutions to get the economy back on track.

We can start by undoing ineffective government policies and programs. Washington politicians, including some Republicans, have been unwilling to address glaringly obvious waste and duplication. Almost every policy that has come out of Washington in the last decade has increased spending and grown government.

Presidents and Congress have added hundreds of questionable programs, giving little thought as to whether or not they actually work.

Democrats continue to claim that cutting federal programs and spending will hurt the poor, disadvantaged, and elderly. They even insist that less government spending will hurt the economy. But the opposite is true. Reforming and streamlining federal services will deliver more cost-efficient and effective services to the people who need them. And less government spending will leave more money in the private sector, which will actually create jobs.

Our future is certainly in jeopardy if we don't make some hard choices now, but spending cuts and reforming federal programs need not be a doomsday scenario for Americans. All Americans—young, old, the poor, literally everyone—will be better off if we reduce the size of the federal government, limit the scope of its power, and restore constitutional government.

In addition to cutting obvious waste and duplicative programs, many government services must be reformed so that they reflect the integral principles that first created American exceptionalism—decentralized political power and individualism. These principles must guide the development of effective government programs. They are real "freedom solutions"—and employing them will ignite economic growth, create new jobs, and eliminate federal deficits.

Despite the conventional wisdom in Washington, the solutions to America's economic and fiscal problems are not simply a matter of what the federal government must do—but what it must let go of. We don't need more "solutions" like the massive government stimulus program that actually hurt our economy by adding trillions to our national debt; we don't need more government control of health care and education; we don't need a federal government that limits energy development and restricts credit to small businesses.

No, we need to let freedom work.

Despite the claims of many liberals, freedom has not failed to work in America—politicians have failed to let it work. We can and must re-create a framework of public policy that will restore America's prosperity and promise. There are numerous reforms and policy changes that don't require new federal spending, just more freedom—more free people, free markets, and free states.

And it is not more government but these freedom solutions that will restore America's greatness.

### Freedom from Debt: The Balanced Budget Amendment to the Constitution

It is an absolute certainty that Washington politicians will bankrupt America if they are not required by law to balance the federal budget. When this idea was proposed during the debt ceiling debate, President Obama responded that he and Congress don't need a constitutional amendment to make them do their jobs.

Yes you do, Mr. President.

No matter which party is in charge, without a balanced budget amendment to force their hand, Congress will continue to spend more than it brings in. The American people must force Washington leaders to finally balance the books. President Obama can call this unnecessary all he wants—but history and experience say otherwise.

America is drowning in debt, yet Obama sent a budget to Congress in 2011 that would nearly double what we owe in ten years. This is quintessential head-in-the-sand Washington thinking. America cannot borrow another $10 trillion. There is not that much credit available in the whole world. If we plan government spending based on the assumption that we can continue to borrow more than $1 trillion a year, America will soon experience a complete economic meltdown.

Families, businesses, organizations, and states must balance their budgets. If they don't, they will go bankrupt. It is inevitable and as certain as the sun rising every day. Yet in Washington, President Obama and the Democrats have called the idea of balancing the federal budget extreme. Such broken logic is as maddening as it is frightening.

The first and most important freedom solution is addressing the piling on of even more mountains of debt. Every child born today already owes more than $45,000 to the federal government, and if this figure is calculated based on Americans who will actually pay federal income taxes, the debt per taxpayer is actually closer to $100,000. This does not even include the trillions of dollars in unfunded liabilities for Social Security and Medicare that currently exist and continue to worsen. Unless we act now to force fiscal sanity upon Washington, future generations of Americans will unquestionably face drastically higher taxes, diminished opportunities, and significantly less freedom. We must have a strong balanced budget amendment like the one proposed by Senator Mike Lee and cosponsored by every Republican senator in 2011. In addition to forcing Congress to limit spending to revenues, it would limit federal spending to 18 percent of the Gross Domestic

Product, or GDP (the historical average of spending versus the total size of the economy). If tax revenues fall, Congress would have to reduce spending accordingly to balance its books. And perhaps most important, Senator Lee's amendment would require a two-thirds supermajority in both Houses of Congress before tax increases could be used to balance the budget.

Liberals worry that a balanced budget amendment would seriously hamper Congress's ability to spend. They're right. Actually passing a balanced budget amendment to the Constitution requires a two-thirds vote of both houses of Congress and approval by at least two thirds of the states. A CNN poll in July revealed that 74 percent of Americans support a balanced budget amendment. Now is the time to allow Americans the ability to decide if balancing the federal budget really is an extreme idea.

## Education Freedom

American taxpayers spend approximately $550 billion a year on K–12 public education; more than any other government program and more per child than any other country spends on education. Taxpayers also spend another $373 billion for higher education every year—yet American students are becoming less competitive with almost every other industrialized nation.[1]

The federal government provides less than 10 percent of the total funding for public education, but federal mandates add more than a third to the cost of operating public schools. Federal funding is divided into dozens of programs, but the federal government only provides part of the funding for these programs.

States and local schools are required to match partial federal funding and administer the programs—if they don't, they simply won't receive the money needed for operating. This mandate depletes local funds and requires massive amounts of paperwork. After public schools spend all of their local and state money to implement federal programs, and teachers spend hours filling out federal paperwork, there is little money or time left to focus on individual student needs, much less any innovative programs.

Since Washington first implemented such collectivist policies concerning education in the 1970s, the quality of American public education has declined consistently relative to other nations. The high school dropout rate is now between one third and one half, depending on who is measuring—the government or a citizen watchdog group. Over their lifetime, a high school dropout costs society approximately $240,000 due to lower tax contributions, higher reliance on Medicaid and Medicare, higher rates of crime, and higher reliance on welfare.[2]

Poor-quality public education is a huge problem for America—and it is also a serious threat to freedom. Since the principles of freedom depend on the character and capabilities of individuals, the development and education of children are important goals for a free society—which also means education is simply too important to be conceded to the inefficient bureaucracy characteristic of our federal government.

Government cannot instill in children the character and discipline they need to become productive citizens. These must come from good parents and community-based schools that reflect the morals and principles individuals need to be successful in life.

High-quality, publicly funded education should be a priority for local and state governments, but public education should not be synonymous with government-run schools. Public funding of education can be justified because individuals with character and skills benefit society as a whole. But there is a big difference between supporting taxpayer-funded education and demanding that the federal government and teachers' unions run our schools.

America's public schools should not expect the continuing gravy train of federal funding. With large budget deficits forecast for decades and the national debt growing proportionately, increases in federal spending for education are highly unlikely. It is also more likely that public education will receive a smaller share of federal dollars.

If the federal government reduces its funding for education and keeps in place all its federal programs and mandates, this will make public education even worse. But what if the federal government lets go of its near monopoly on public education? What if the federal government requires that states guarantee equal opportunity for all students and then allows the states to design their own education systems?

I am one of the sponsors of the A-PLUS Act, which has been introduced in both houses of Congress. This legislation would allow states to operate much like charter schools; they could agree to certain standards while still being allowed the flexibility to run their schools the way they want. Federal money would be block-granted to these charter states instead of being divided among multiple programs. If states don't meet federal standards, they would have to return to the federal regimen.

A-PLUS would allow states to be innovative and, more important, to adapt their schools to the needs of students. Successes in one state would be copied and improved upon by other states.

Competition for the best schools would raise the standards for schools throughout the nation. This could be a revolution in improving the quality of education American students receive, while the size and cost of the Department of Education could be significantly reduced.

Democrats and teachers unions vigorously oppose A-PLUS because it would reduce their power and control of the federal government. But this legislation could pass if governors, state legislators, businesses, and parents demanded the right to develop better schools.

And states don't have to wait for Congress to approve their right to innovate. A 2002 Supreme Court decision, *Zelman v. Simmons-Harris*, confirmed that states have the right to provide vouchers for students to attend private schools. Democrats have made *vouchers* a bad word, claiming they would destroy public schools. What Democrats are really afraid of is that if parents have better choices, their children will escape failing government schools, lessening the liberal stranglehold on education.

Most states now spend more than $10,000 per year for every child in government schools. Even if only half of this figure—$5,000—was given to children as a scholarship to any accredited school, the private sector would explode with innovative choices to meet the needs of a wide variety of students.

Publicly funded scholarships would also lead to significant private-sector investment in America's education. Millions of new education consumers would entice American investors and entrepreneurs to create specialized schools to compete for a share of one of the world's largest and most profitable new markets. America's best minds would create thousands of new world-class schools at a huge savings to taxpayers.

Democrats often argue that publicly funded education scholarships (that is, vouchers) would drain money from government
schools and lead to the resegregation of schools. This is utter nonsense. It is true that with a portable scholarship program, government schools would have to become more competitive or be
replaced by better, less expensive schools.

But thankfully, school segregation is gone forever. This generation of American students is so far past the thought of segregation that for the overwhelming majority of America's youth,
any hint of discrimination is repugnant. Liberals continue to raise
the specter of institutionalized racism in places like public education, where strong modern attitudes against it will unquestionably
prevent it from ever reemerging.

That said, it is true that government schools have been ineffective at preparing African-Americans and Hispanics to be successful in a free society. Poor and minority students are the greatest
casualties of a one-size-fits-all government education system,
which Democrats ironically claim is supposed to benefit them. It is
time to replace government schools with independent schools that
work for all students and for America.

Students have a wide variety of aptitudes and learning styles.
This is not a product of race or gender; it is because all human
beings are different. Unless America creates a diverse set of learning environments, millions of students will continue to be left
behind. The government cannot create the system of specialized
and individualized schools necessary to give every student the
opportunity to succeed.

Education freedom would help America's fiscal and economic
problems now and in the future. It would also reduce federal

spending, strengthen our culture and workforce, and lead to higher tax revenues.

## Health-Care Freedom

America has one of the best health-care systems in the world but some of the unhealthiest citizens. Despite making health care cheap or "free" for a large number of Americans, our population is plagued with obesity, drug use, depression, and other pathologies that reduce productivity and add significantly to the cost of health services.

Nearly half of Americans today use a government health-care plan: Medicare, Medicaid, and military or veterans' plans. Medicaid offers virtually free health care for the poor and will soon be the health-care plan for millions of Americans who will be forced into ObamaCare. Despite access to no-cost or low-cost health care, America's poor are plagued with debilitating physical and psychological conditions that are caused by their unhealthy lifestyles.

Free access to health care does not lead to good health. When people are relieved of the responsibility of choosing and paying for their health insurance and health care, they often also feel like they are relieved of responsibility for their own health. Independence and the self-reliance that accompanies it go right out the window. There simply has to be a better balance between personal responsibility and public assistance with health care.

America is currently on a course toward socialized medicine, where the entire health-care system will be controlled by the federal government. Unless ObamaCare is repealed, more than two-thirds of Americans will be on a government health plan within five years. Government health plans do not pay doctors and hospitals enough to cover their costs, so more and more costs will be shifted to patients with private insurance. The cost of private insurance will continue to rise, forcing more Americans onto government plans. Soon the private health insurance market will collapse, and Americans will have only one choice—government health care.

Freedom solutions in health care can provide better choices, improve the health status of Americans, and stop the socialization of one-sixth of America's economy. Using the principles of freedom—decentralized political power and individualism—every American can have access to health plans they can afford, can own, and keep from job to job and through retirement. Americans who take the responsibility to buy their health insurance should also have a legal guarantee that their insurance cannot be cancelled or the cost increased because of a health condition that occurs after the insurance was purchased.

Until the tax code is reformed to create a low, flat rate, individuals who buy their own health insurance should receive the same tax deductions as employers. We should also break up the state-by-state insurance monopolies and allow individuals to buy health insurance across state lines. Giving states the ability to compete would lower the cost of health insurance by creating a highly competitive, national insurance market for individuals.

Small employers and organizations should be free to join together to buy health insurance at lower prices. Today, federal laws give large corporations a huge advantage over small businesses and individuals. There is no good reason why individual Americans, small businesses, churches, and volunteer organizations should not be free to cooperate together to buy health insurance.

Additionally, frivolous lawsuits against doctors and hospitals must be stopped. Hospital administrators tell me up to a third of their costs can be attributed to defensive medicine, additional staff, paperwork, liability insurance, and the legal costs related to the threat of lawsuits. Individual doctors pay tens of thousands of dollars a year for medical malpractice insurance to insulate themselves against the high cost of even one lawsuit.

Of course, patients should always have recourse against doctors and hospitals that harm them through negligence or incompetence. But the legal system is now set up to the advantage of plaintiff lawyers who cost good doctors and hospitals thousands of dollars by simply threatening a lawsuit. Even if doctors spend hundreds of thousands in legal costs defending themselves—and even if they win—they do not recoup their legal costs. It is easier and cheaper to pay thousands and sometimes millions of dollars to settle a case. Lawyers get rich, the cost of health care goes up— and America suffers for it.

We must have a loser-pays tort system in America like almost every other modern country. Under this system people are free to file a lawsuit for any reason, but if they lose, they have to pay the legal costs of the winning party. This would eliminate the no-risk lawsuit environment we now have in this country, which threatens not only our health-care system but virtually every employer.

Americans should be free to buy their health insurance, and employers should be free to contribute to the cost of these plans. Individuals should also be free to have a health savings account and high-deductible health plans if they choose. Employers could contribute to individual HSAs, and employees should be allowed to use the money in their HSAs to pay for their own health insurance (unbelievably, the federal government now prohibits this commonsense idea).

When an employee changes jobs, their insurance and HSA should go with them. And when they retire, Americans should be able to choose between government Medicare or an annual subsidy to help pay for their private plan. Americans should also be encouraged to keep their private health insurance in retirement.

If they knew they would have the opportunity to keep their private health plan when they retire, many young workers would contract with insurance companies for individual whole life health insurance that would guarantee set rates and renewals regardless of age or health condition.

The cost of the Medicare program could be reduced substantially over time if Americans were given the option of taking a premium support subsidy that helps pay for a private policy in retirement.

Every state should have a high-risk health insurance pool for citizens with preexisting health conditions. Some states have already contracted with insurance companies to provide lower-cost, managed-care health insurance for individuals who can't find affordable insurance on the open market.

High-risk pools are a better solution for patients with preexisting conditions than mandates, which require insurance companies to accept these patients at market rates. These mandates increase the cost of private health insurance for everyone, because when healthy people know they can wait to buy insurance until after they get sick, fewer will buy insurance.

Americans should not be required to buy insurance—but they should be required to pay their own health-care bills. Low-income or disabled Americans should have some assistance in purchasing their own insurance, but everyone should share in the responsibility to buy their health insurance and pay for their health care.

State laws should be strengthened to allow doctors and hospitals legal recourse against patients who do not have insurance or the means to pay their bills. Once Americans realize that they will be responsible for their medical bills, most will take the responsibility of buying health insurance.

## Energy Freedom

When President Obama took office, the price of a gallon of gasoline was $1.83. Two years later gas prices had nearly doubled to more than $3.60. Part of the reason for this: the Obama administration had delayed drilling and mining permits, dramatically expanded nuisance environmental regulations, and bypassed Congress to begin regulating $CO_2$.

President Obama's policies resulted in thousands of lost jobs in the energy sector, and higher gas prices drained billions from the American economy. Yet despite a worsening economy and stubbornly high unemployment, the Obama administration wouldn't relent—and the administration continued to sacrifice jobs to satisfy the environmentalist left.

The United States has some of the largest energy reserves in the world. Recent discoveries of natural gas and shale oil and gas could jump-start America's economy and provide us with low-emission fuel for more than one hundred years—that is, if the federal government would allow states and private companies to develop these resources.

In 2011, I joined a dozen Republican senators in support of Senator David Vitter's 3-D energy legislation. The three "D's" represent Domestic jobs, Domestic energy, and Deficit reduction. Without spending one dime of taxpayer money, this legislation, if implemented, would create two million jobs, $10 trillion in economic activity, and $2 trillion in federal tax receipts over the next thirty years. It would also make America more energy independent.

Vitter's 3-D legislation would require the Secretary of the Interior to open up deep-sea oil and gas development in the Atlantic Ocean. It would open the huge oil reserves in Alaska, known as ANWR, and it would expedite permits to develop onshore energy reserves in several states.

The American Energy Alliance estimates that development of the United States' energy reserves in the Atlantic Ocean (the Outer Continental Shelf) would create 1.8 million new full-time jobs, $8 trillion in GDP growth, and $2.2 trillion in additional federal tax receipts. According to Wharton Econometrics Forecasting Associates, developing oil reserves in ANWR would create 730,000 jobs, $114 billion in federal royalty revenue, and another $95 billion in additional federal corporate income tax revenue.

So what are we waiting for?

America's current energy policies are not only detrimental to our economy; they are a threat to our national security. Our dependence on foreign oil is the largest contributor to our trade deficit and makes our very survival dependent on the whims of many nations that are not our friends. If there was any serious economic, political, and national security sanity in the White House, domestic energy development would be America's most urgent and immediate priority.

## Tax Freedom

America's tax code is a monumental drag on job creation and economic growth. Citizens and businesses spend millions of hours every year, wasting billions of dollars in economic productivity, just filling out tax forms. American manufactured products are at a disadvantage because our exports, unlike our trading partners, include the cost of domestic taxes. Politicians have campaigned for decades on fixing the tax code, but once in Washington, members of Congress always seem to forget about their tax reform promises. Why?

Manipulating the tax code, creating loopholes and credits for favored constituents and campaign supporters, is part of the culture of Washington. Big corporations complain about the tax code, but they have too much invested in the status quo to support real tax reform. Democrats also complain about the tax code, but actively oppose efforts to create a simple flat-tax system that would force more Americans to share in the cost of big government.

During the heated debt limit debate in 2011, Democrats demanded that big corporations and rich Americans pay their fair share of taxes. They insisted that any debt deal should increase taxes on the wealthy. Republicans countered that higher taxes would hurt the economy. But what is the truth about who pays their fair share of taxes?

President Obama regularly insists that individual Americans making over $200,000 and married couples raking in more than $250,000 should pay higher taxes. This group comprises 3 percent of taxpayers, who earn 30 percent of the nation's income and pay 52 percent of all federal income taxes. Three percent of Americans now pay over half of all federal income taxes, while over half of Americans pay no federal income tax at all.

Sixty-five percent of married couples earning above $250,000 annually include small business income as part of their personal tax returns. This means that the President's proposed tax hikes on the "rich" could affect 37 million workers and nearly half of all potential new jobs. The Heritage Foundation estimates that Obama's tax increases would cost small businesses $74 billion annually, which translates into the potential loss of 1.2 million jobs.

Obama's liberal plan to make the "rich" pay their "fair share" would actually have the real-life effect of hurting countless Americans who desperately need jobs.

It is important for Americans to know what the "rich" do with their money. Consumer spending makes up about 70 percent of America's economy, and America's top 5 percent of earners account for 37 percent of all consumer spending. Those making more than $150,000 spend an average of $125,000 per year—enough to support two and a half middle-class jobs.[3]

The top 10 percent of families provide 64 percent of all major investment assets to the economy.[4] In 2008, the 3 percent of Americans making more than $200,000 also accounted for 36 percent of all charitable contributions. Raising taxes on these Americans will reduce investments in our economy, hurt thousands of small businesses, reduce charitable contributions, and simply give Washington more money to waste.

This will not do.

It costs businesses approximately $63,000 a year to create one middle-class job that pays $41,000. Obama's tax increases would take $74 billion from businesses, which could translate into

1.2 million lost jobs. Do we really want to take more money from the people who are creating jobs and give it to the bureaucrats who have created the $15 billion national debt?

Tax reform should not be based on taking more money from America's job creators. It should be based on the benefits of creating lower, flatter rates with fewer deductions and loopholes. Currently 10 percent of Americans pay 70 percent of all federal income taxes. This creates extreme fluctuations in tax revenues that would not exist under a flatter tax system.

During a recent recession, GDP declined less than 1 percent from 2007 to 2009, yet because our tax system is weighted so heavily on investors and business profits, total income tax revenues plummeted more than 20 percent. America desperately needs a fair and flat tax code.

There are numerous tax reform ideas that should be considered. Consumption tax proposals, such as the Fair Tax, would eliminate all income, payroll, and business taxes, and replace them with a 23 percent national sales tax. The elimination of business taxes would make America one of the best places in the world to manufacture goods. Rebates would be provided to insulate poor Americans against higher taxes, and the rich, who are the nation's largest consumers, would pay disproportionately more taxes. But all citizens would participate at least in a small way in paying for the cost of government.

There are other reform proposals that include a flatter income tax system such as Representative Paul Ryan's Road Map for Tax Reform. His plan would create a two-tier income tax system with the first $50,000 of individual income ($100,000 for married couples) taxed at 10 percent. Income above these levels would be taxed at 25 percent. Almost all tax deductions and credits would be eliminated except for a $12,500 standard deduction for individuals and $25,000 for joint tax filers. Ryan's plan also creates a simple business tax that excludes taxes on exports.

Republicans have developed and introduced numerous tax reform proposals that simplify and flatten tax rates, but Democrats continue to demand that the tax code take even more money from investors, business owners, and upper-income Americans. Liberals are entirely comfortable with the broken tax system status quo simply because they benefit too much from it—and we will not fix our tax code with Obama in the White House and Democrats running the Senate.

## Retirement Freedom: Social Security Reform

Currently, all working Americans are required to pay 12.4 percent of their income (for the first $106,800 in earnings) into the Social Security system (employers pay half and the individual pays half). These taxes pay the benefits of current retirees. None of the money is actually saved for the individual who pays the taxes but is put into the general fund and spent immediately by reckless politicians.

When Americans begin collecting Social Security benefits (between ages 62 and 66), they receive an annual income that, for most, is just above the poverty level. Unfortunately, Social Security's pay-as-you-go system no longer works. Mathematically, there are simply not enough workers paying the taxes needed to send the monthly Social Security checks to the growing ranks of retired Americans.

Social Security is effectively broke. Democrats won't admit

this glaring truth because it hurts them politically. While there are $2.6 trillion in government bonds in the Social Security Trust Fund, these bonds would have to be sold and converted to public debt to generate the cash needed to pay benefits. This means the United States will have to borrow billions of dollars every month to keep our promises to seniors. We found out during the debt limit debate in 2011 that Social Security is hardly a guarantee; Obama said there might not be enough money to pay monthly benefits unless the United States continued to borrow money.

Social Security can be saved without cutting benefits to seniors if politicians are willing to give workers and seniors more choices based on individual freedom and responsibility. One idea is to give all retired and retiring seniors with alternative sources of income the option of taking a tax-free lump sum payment equal to one half of their projected actuarial payout.

If my estimated payout at sixty-five years old over the next ten or fifteen years is $250,000, I would gladly take a lump sum of $125,000 the day I retired. If only a small percent of seniors took this option, it would save the country billions of dollars. This arrangement would also encourage younger workers to save more so they could cash out of Social Security when they retire.

Another freedom option would be to allow workers over fifty to opt out of future Social Security benefits. These workers would keep their portion of Social Security taxes (6.2 percent) for the remainder of their working lives if they purchased an annuity that guaranteed a base income when they retired. This could save individuals thousands of dollars a year and spare the government billions of future Social Security payments.

The Social Security system should begin a long-term transition from a pay-as-you-go defined-benefit pension plan to a fully funded defined-contribution plan. Most businesses and many states have moved away from retirement pension plans that guarantee a specific level of benefit and replaced them with 401(k)-style plans.

Representative Ryan proposed a Social Security reform plan that allows today's workers to contribute a small part of their Social Security taxes into personal 401(k)-style accounts. These accounts would work within the current system to guarantee promised benefits. Over time, workers would be allowed to contribute a larger and larger share of their Social Security taxes into personal accounts. Under this plan, when my grandchildren retire, their Social Security retirement account would be fully funded, and the U.S. government would not have to keep borrowing money to pay their benefits.

There are many other ideas to fix Social Security by giving Americans more choices and more freedom. These options, however, will not be acceptable to Democrats because they reduce dependency on the government and decrease the power of the federal government.

## More Freedom for States

Many federal functions should be devolved to the states to improve services and reduce costs. Medicaid funds should be block-granted to states and states given the flexibility to reform programs.

The Department of Transportation should be downsized to focus on maintaining federal roads. Instead of 18 cents in taxes from every gallon of gas coming to the federal government, only 3 cents is needed. The rest should be controlled by the states to build local and state infrastructure. States should agree to certain safety standards but otherwise be free from federal mandates and union requirements.

Numerous environmental, agriculture, and commerce functions should be delegated to the states, and federal agencies should be downsized and consolidated to save money and improve services.

Such state solutions are no-brainers, and there's nothing logically that should stop us—except Democrats—from enacting these legislative proposals as soon as possible.

## Summary

Politicians have long claimed that federal spending must grow every year or Americans would suffer. They have gotten their way, spending the nation into suffocating levels of debt. Yet, despite decades of promises and fearmongering, they have not made life better for citizens. In many cases, federal involvement and irresponsible spending have made things worse.

Cutting waste and duplication, rolling back onerous and expensive regulations, and implementing freedom solutions will reduce spending and debt, create prosperity, and expand freedom for all Americans. The only sacrifices that will have to be made are by politicians and some government workers who will need to find private-sector jobs. These are sacrifices that we must demand they make. The average American taxpayer has been asked to make all the sacrifices for far too long.

These commonsense solutions will never be adopted unless the Democrats are defeated in 2012. Democrats will never agree to reduce the size, scope, and spending of the federal government, so they must be replaced.

Getting rid of big government will necessarily mean getting rid of its greatest protectors.

## Share the Truth

- We can cut the size and spending of the federal government and the national debt while improving services and choices for Americans.
- The first priority is to pass, and for states to ratify, a balanced budget amendment to the Constitution.
- There are many freedom solutions that can cut costs and improve education, health care, transportation, and other government services.
- Opening up America's energy resources would create millions of jobs, billions of dollars of new tax revenue, and could help reduce America's debt.
- These commonsense solutions will never be adopted unless Democrats are replaced in the White House and Congress.

# 7

# The Right Message
to America

## Introduction by Political Consultant
## Dr. Frank Luntz

My career is in language. For over twenty years, I've helped senators and CEOs identify the right message to reach the hearts and minds of their audience. My counsel has a common theme: *It's not what YOU say; it's what THEY HEAR that really matters.*

Then, after the 2008 election, everything changed. Now, while *what they hear* still matters, *how well you listen* matters far more. Effective communication now requires you to be the voice of the people you wish to lead.

This is the hallmark of the Tea Party's impact on American politics—a strategic imperative to be accountable to the people. In fact, the number one attribute conservatives want from Washington is for the politicians to listen to us—*the people who elected them.*

More than they desire a balanced budget amendment, more than they want constitutional government, and even more than they want lower taxes, what conservatives want most is accountability in their government. Thanks to the Tea Party, this is happening—and conservatives have now become the chief agents of accountability in American politics.

In fact, there is a truth that remains a mystery to the

Washington establishment but is an open fact to those of us who survey public opinion professionally:

Tea Party values *are* American values. Their demand for accountability is shared by wide majorities of Americans. Across the political spectrum, Americans seek an end to wasteful Washington spending and to replace it with a government that lives within its means. They want a government that respects the rule of law and is more efficient and effective, not bigger and more controlling.

The best political language speaks to the common sense of common Americans. It is informed, active, and demands a seat at the table. There are a dozen essential ways to communicate to this new generation of conservative activist. Here are the twelve words and phrases that together comprise the Right Message for 2012:

1. *Freedom.* For decades, freedom was a rallying cry for people on the right and a blatant partisan, political appeal for everyone else. No longer. With half of America feeling less free today than they did five years ago, fighting for freedom—and against those who would deny it—is the single most powerful organizing principle today.

2. *Accountability.* This is the sharpest word in the tool kit, and it gets sharper with every promise President Obama breaks. The American people want a government that does what it promises—nothing less and

nothing more. No more budget gimmicks. No more accounting tricks. No more empty promises.

3. *I say what I mean and I mean what I say.* If accountability is what people want from their government, straight talk is what they want from their elected representatives. Put down your notes, dump the teleprompter, come out from behind the podium, look your audience straight in the eye, and tell them exactly what you think.

4. *No excuses.* Americans are fed up with politicians who are full of promises one day and excuses the next. When you tell audiences you won't make—and won't accept—any excuses, they'll know you're serious about getting things done.

5. *The simple truth.* The American people are looking for leaders who will simplify, clarify, and level with them. The simple truth is that Washington cannot continue to spend more than it takes in. The simple truth is that a great country needs great schools. Delivering the simple truth, good or bad, is what Americans want to hear.

6. *Control.* The words and phrases up to now have been about the elected. This word is about the governed. We are asking—demanding—more control over our schools, our health care, our retirement, our lives. It comes down to a simple question: "Who do you trust more to control the most important decisions in your life...you, or a Washington bureaucrat?" (Note to

communicators: asking questions is putting your audience in control.)

7. *Government takeover.* This phrase entered the public lexicon in 2009, and it is even more powerful today. The vast majority of Americans are outraged over a government takeover of health care, financial services, automotive companies, student loans—the list goes on and on. They are tired of Washington passing laws that create a culture where people at the top get a bailout, people at the bottom get a handout, and everyone else gets the bill.

8. *Enforcement, not expansion.* The American people know we have more than enough laws and regulations on the books to keep the public safe and hold corporations and individuals accountable. They want the government to run more efficiently, not regulate more aggressively.

9. *Families have tightened their belts. So should government.* It is infuriating for families and small business owners to be asked to pay more for an inefficient, expanding government when they have had to cut back. Everyone except government has learned to do more with less.

10. *Empower job creators—don't punish them.* The 2012 election will see the most blatant attempt at class warfare ever waged by the Left. "Tax the rich" is and will continue to be the rallying cry among the antibusiness crowd, but don't take the bait. Instead, recast the

debate: the Left seeks tax increases that punish the innovators, entrepreneurs, and small business owners upon whom we are relying to lead us out of the recession.

11. *Common sense.* It's not "balance," as President Obama would say, or "compromise" that Americans crave. It's a return to good, old-fashioned common sense. From promoting "legal reform" (a more accessible term than "tort reform") to "opportunity scholarships" in education (more popular than "vouchers"), Americans crave a commonsense approach to the issues of the day.

12. *America.* It may seem so obvious, but people who appeal to American values or the American Dream are far more popular than those who call for government involvement or intervention. For tens of millions of Americans, it really is them (Washington) vs. us (America). And thanks to Jim DeMint, America is winning.

These are serious times, and they require a serious commitment to inform, educate, and communicate. If you don't think the American Dream hangs in the balance, ask yourself two questions:

Do I have a higher quality of life than my parents did when they were my age? *(Fully 70 percent of Americans say yes to this question.)*

Do you think your children will have a higher quality of life than you when they are your age? *(Only 34 percent of Americans say yes.)*

*This* is what the 2012 election is all about—a future of freedom and opportunity or a future of debt, doubt, and despair. The organizations and candidates who seize these messages will show the American people they're listening, that they *just plain get it.* And as a result, they'll seize control of the future.

F rank Luntz *listens* to thousands of Americans every year about what they think is right and wrong with this country, and he understands what they expect from their elected leaders. Many Washington politicians, however, seem to think Americans are stupid. These politicians talk down to voters, say one thing at a press conference then do the exact opposite when they vote. And these hypocrites are harshly critical of anyone who has the gall to point out their duplicity.

Republicans must convince Americans that we say what we mean and mean what we say. The American people have every reason in the world not to trust anything that anyone from Washington says. Therefore, we must be honest and straightforward (no Washington doublespeak) to win the trust of the majority of Americans. Voters have to believe we are telling the truth when we say, "It's now or never to save America." Our message must be clear and persuasive.

The good news is it's easy to sound truthful when you're telling the truth. The bad news is, penetrating the clutter, the dishonesty, and the media's ruthless tricks will be difficult.

After the debt limit debate concluded with a supposed grand bargain between congressional leaders and the President, Democrats and members of the media expressed outrage that Tea Party activists had held the nation hostage, "held a gun to the heads of Republicans" and acted like terrorists.

Republican congressmen and senators who insisted on a balanced budget and supported the Cut, Cap, and Balance legislation were often referred to by the media as "Tea Party Republicans." They used "Tea Party" as a pejorative to suggest Republicans were being controlled by a small, extreme right-wing group of political operatives.

But these critics didn't know anything about the Tea Party and certainly weren't qualified to speak for them. Democrats, who are often controlled by a few union bosses and large financiers like George Soros, can't even conceive of a genuine grassroots citizens' movement that doesn't want anything from government—except freedom from it.

There is no one Tea Party group or Tea Party leader. The Tea Party is a bottom-up operation, not top-down, that differs from state to state, city to city, neighborhood to neighborhood. The label can rightly be used to describe thousands of citizen groups who are concerned about—or actually fearful of—the out-of-control spending, borrowing, debt, and growth of the federal government. They demand a balanced budget and a return to constitutional limited government not because they are extreme, but because they fear a truly extreme federal government.

Tea Party groups range in size from a few scattered individuals to a few thousand with strong organization. They are composed of a diverse mix of Americans representing a broad cross-section of political ideologies. The Tea Party includes libertarians, Democrats, Republicans, independents, and many people who have not been involved in politics at all. They are united by fiscal and economic issues, and they are strongly opposed to the federal government's ever-increasing intervention into all areas of the private sector.

For every official Tea Party member, there are hundreds of Americans who agree with their concerns and goals. It is hardly a small movement. Over 70 percent of Americans believe the federal government should balance its budget, and nearly that many also supported the Cut, Cap, and Balance legislation to control spending, which would finally put America on a path toward balancing its budget.

The Tea Party doesn't represent a small fringe but a broad coalition of Americans increasingly united against an oppressive federal government intent on bankrupting our nation.

## A Message That Connects with Freedom-Loving Americans

Unfortunately, too many Americans are dependent on the government and simply want more from it. These citizens are naturally more susceptible to scare tactics and manipulation by the Democrats and the media. Republicans should not attempt to obscure our goals or dilute our message in an attempt to win these voters. This would be a losing proposition from the outset. But although we cannot win their votes now, we can fight to set them free.

As John Adams once wrote to James Warren:

Popularity was never my mistress, nor was I ever, or shall I ever be a popular man. But one thing I know, a man must be sensible of the errors of the people, and upon his guard against them, and must run the risk of their displeasure sometimes, or he will never do them any good in the long run.[1]

Republicans must understand that most of our audience is made up of those Americans who still have a spark of the fire of freedom in their hearts. Despite several generations of voters being educated in collectivist government schools, with little teaching about the exceptional nature of our country, most Americans still instinctively respond to the call of freedom.

Competing and contradictory messages will continue to come from Democrats and the media, but Republicans can ignite the flames of freedom for the majority of Americans if we insist on being *honest and bold*. We do not need different messages for women, the young, old, Hispanics, and African-Americans. The message of freedom and opportunity will attract all voters who are willing to work and compete for a share of the American Dream, and who are ready to restore this country's greatness.

The right message begins with the right policies. Republicans must convince Americans that we are serious about fiscal discipline and sincere about reducing the size of the federal government. We must also counter Democrats' claims that reducing spending will hurt America's children, seniors, and disadvantaged.

The facts are on our side—but the media is not.

History and experience tell us that America is in economic trouble. This is not alarmism or hyperbole. Years of reckless spending and centralization of power in Washington have crippled our economy and put us on a course toward bankruptcy. President Obama's policies have made a bad situation much worse, and he seems clueless about how to turn things around.

Government incompetence and waste, costly and paralyzing regulations on businesses, high tax rates and an incomprehensible tax code, ObamaCare and the Dodd-Frank takeover of our financial institutions—all of this continues to bring our economy to its knees. Collectivist social policies and entitlements have damaged this country's characteristic spirit of individualism and forced a near majority of Americans into dependency on the federal government.

But incredibly—despite the devastating impact of Obama's policies—nearly half of Americans still support his reelection. Those who know better must be ready to fight for freedom in 2012—because it really is now or never.

### Be Positive: American Exceptionalism Is Still Working

There is every reason for Americans to be optimistic about our future. America is still the greatest, strongest, most prosperous, and most compassionate nation in history. The principles that made us exceptional are still at work today, but they have been diminished by a massive federal government that has been systematically destroying the core philosophies and values that made America great.

The centralization of political power has largely replaced the principles of constitutional limited government. Collectivist social policies and dependency-creating entitlements have weakened our culture of individual freedom and responsibility. But America's best days can still be ahead of us—if we can find the will to reverse the federal policies that have brought us to the brink.

## We Must Help Americans Understand How Bad Federal Policies Have Hurt Our Country

Obama didn't create America's problems, but he has made them much worse. The concentration of federal power expanded significantly after World War II through the creation of Social Security and the expansion of welfare. The creation of Medicare decades later by President Lyndon Johnson continued the path toward government centralization. Social Security and Medicare serve important purposes for seniors—but they also had the effect of making people dependent. Now, of course, millions of Americans are dependent on these programs. Also, America's welfare programs have trapped millions more in generational poverty and dependency on government.

As the federal government grew well beyond its constitutional boundaries, so did wasteful Washington spending, fraud, and corruption. Excessive government regulation began to stifle America's economic growth and our debt grew exponentially.

President Obama will add about $6 trillion to the national debt during his first term in office—more than any other President in history. Obama has also essentially taken over American's healthcare and financial systems. Under this President, federal agencies have issued hundreds of new regulations, costing the economy trillions of dollars. Unemployment has increased, gas prices have doubled, the number of food stamp recipients has grown nearly 40 percent—food stamps are now administered to over 45 million Americans—and home prices continue to decline.

And President Obama still says his policies are working!

## Freedom Solutions Can Restore America's Greatness

Too many Americans have been willing to give up too many freedoms in return for government promises of more security. But it is a false security. Americans have given up 12.4 percent of their income throughout their working lives for a Social Security system that is now on the verge of bankruptcy. We already know that during the debt limit debate, Obama revealed how secure seniors really are—when the President declared Social Security checks might not go out unless the federal government was allowed to borrow more money.

Americans have also given up 2.5 percent of their income in return for the promise of Medicare government health insurance. Unfortunately, Medicare is also broke. This virtually bankrupt system now pays physicians less than what it actually costs for patient visits. This cannot endure, and changes must be made to guarantee that seniors have access to quality health care.

Chairman of the Joint Chiefs of Staff Mike Mullen has said that more than anything else, "the most significant threat to our national security is our debt." He's right. The greatest threat to both America's freedom and security continues to be our out-of-control spending. Getting control of our debt begins with eliminating wasteful federal programs and reducing the size of the federal government. This can be accomplished in large part by returning many of the federal government's current functions to the states and the people. Regulations must be drastically reduced to allow our economy to grow. And federal policies should be revamped, decentralized, and reassessed to promote individual responsibility—and with it, more freedom.

Younger workers can be given better options concerning Social Security and Medicare without cutting benefits for today's seniors. Education, transportation, and welfare programs must be returned to the states. Energy exploration and development must be unshackled from government's handcuffs. The tax code should be made flat and simple. The Federal Reserve must be refocused on sound monetary policy and restricted from reckless interventions into our economy.

There are many more federal programs and policies that must be eliminated, changed, and delegated to the states—and make no mistake: every American will be better off if we make these commonsense changes. We can also count on the Democrats using every Republican solution as an opportunity to frighten Americans. But despite what they throw at us, we can and must simplify our message of limited government and freedom in a way that will inspire Americans.

## The New Republican Message: Bold, Honest, and Simple

In 2010, Wisconsin Republicans who campaigned on cutting spending and debt won the governor's mansion and a majority in the state legislature. Governor Scott Walker and the Republican majority moved quickly to keep their campaign promises. They reduced spending and debt without raising taxes, and made

Wisconsin a more attractive state for businesses to create jobs. They even had the courage to take on the government unions that had nearly bankrupted the state.

When these Republicans curbed the collective bargaining rights of Wisconsin's state government workers, these workers staged a sit-in at the state capitol, protesting having to pay a small share of their health-care premiums. Union bosses from all around the country recognized these actions as a threat to their monopoly of power over state governments. Union forces organized recall elections to remove from office those Republicans who had the audacity to stand for fiscal sanity rather than being intimidated by union power. But despite unions and liberal organizations spending over $30 million in six small Wisconsin state senate districts—which Obama had won overwhelmingly in 2008—Republicans still won four of the six elections and maintained their Senate majority.

This proved once again that when politicians keep their promises, stand courageously, and offer commonsense solutions, they are usually rewarded by the voters—even in liberal states. The citizens of Wisconsin are not stupid, and neither are the majority of Americans. Most Americans know instinctively that we must change course and are looking for honest politicians who have the courage of their convictions.

Democrats are infamous for their bleeding-heart, fear-mongering, race-baiting, and class-warfare styles of messaging. Republicans must offer a clear contrast to the Democrats' condescending and insulting pandering to special interest groups and dependent voters. We must tell Americans the truth and hope that a majority of Americans will prove the Democrats wrong.

The Democrats are still banking on the American people being stupid—but they're not.

Dr. Frank Luntz offers five steps to communicating effectively with voters. These ideas will work for grassroots organizers, candidates, radio talk show hosts, and anyone trying to recruit more Americans to join the fight for freedom.

### Step 1—Personalize the Consequences of Failure

Forget the political lingo and Washington-speak. For hardworking Americans this isn't about politics; it is about our lives. We're about to lose our country. Our children deserve a future free from crushing taxes and dependency on borrowed money from China. Even more wasteful Washington spending will drain our pockets of hard-earned money and leave our families with even less to spend on our real needs. We must take on the big problems in government now or they will destroy our future.

### Step 2—Personalize the Benefits of Success

Challenge Americans to imagine a better future. Think of what America can achieve if we are free from Washington control and debt. This message is about much more than controlling our irresponsible government—it is about restoring the American Dream. It is true that we are facing great challenges, but this is still America—and Americans don't run from anything. We can, and we will, build a brighter American future for this generation and the next.

### Step 3—Our Government and Elected Leaders Must Be Held Accountable

American families have to balance their checkbooks. Businesses have to balance their books. States have to balance their budgets. Why can't Washington balance its budget? Our government must be accountable to the people. We can't keep spending more than we are bringing in and expect to survive. Americans must demand a constitutional amendment that requires Congress to balance its budget every year. No more excuses: pass a balanced budget amendment to the Constitution. Now.

### Step 4—Americans Deserve the Facts

Americans are sick and tired of politicians who say it's daytime when everyone else sees a full moon overhead. Facts do matter. Obama's stimulus didn't work. ObamaCare didn't reduce the cost of health care. The Democratic takeover of the financial industry did not make credit more available to small businesses or home buyers. The big debt deal of 2011 did not reduce our national debt. Americans deserve fact-based budgeting and policies, and Republicans must re-earn the trust of the American people with total honesty and fact-based communications.

### Step 5—Put People First

Governments are established to serve the people, not vice versa. The American government must be a government of the people, for the people, and by the people. This must be more than a dusty old political slogan—it must be Republicans' commitment to America. United States citizens are paying for a better government than they are getting. We need to throw out self-serving politicians and government unions and, once again, put the American people first.

## Share the Truth

- Voters reward candidates who tell the truth and keep their promises once in office. Republicans must be bold and honest.
- Democrats will continue to mislead and frighten Americans—especially voters who are dependent on the government.
- The Republican message must personalize the issues: this is about people, not politics.
- People must understand the consequences of failure and the benefits of success: we will either lose our country or create a better America.
- Democrats will continue to refuse to hold government accountable. Republicans will make the government accountable to the people.

# 8

# Choosing the Right Messengers to America

# Introduction by Former House Majority Leader Dick Armey

Thomas "Tip" O'Neill used to say that all politics is local. In a representative democracy there is, of course, a responsibility for elected officials to represent their districts or states. But O'Neill had it wrong. Not all politics are local. We must also have leaders committed to the good of the entire country. When members of Congress are elected, they take an oath to support the Constitution—not to bring home the bacon.

The O'Neil philosophy—which existed long before he gave it a catchy tagline—propagated a "me first" attitude among the establishment and has reinforced a "my district first" attitude among voters. The more politicians promised, the more voters expected—and the more politicians had to deliver. As this cycle continued throughout the years, it became increasingly clear to the electorate that federal spending was getting out of control.

It's often difficult, if not impossible, to change the culture in Washington. Frustrated with Washington's refusal to change, in 2009 voters decided to institute some change of their own. Countless Americans came to the disappointing realization that establishment politicians in Washington didn't necessarily know what was best for America, and started to reclaim both the right and responsibility to hold them accountable.

This created a foundation for what would come to be known as the Tea Party class, made up of the sixty-nine fiscal conservatives sent to Washington in the 2009 elections. Rather than simply answering to entrenched party and special interests, Tea Party politicians answer to the people who elected them.

But how did this unusual change of events in Washington occur? By picking the right people to run. The establishment—whether in Washington, D.C., or at the local and state levels—thinks it knows which candidates are the most electable. Their calculations are often based on superficial factors like name identification, access to high-dollar donors, and other characteristics that have very little to do with actual principles. Recognizing this, grassroots activists looked for candidates with a commitment to big ideas and core values like freedom and individual responsibility.

The establishment picked Bob Bennett. The grassroots picked Mike Lee.

The establishment picked Charlie Crist. The grassroots picked Marco Rubio.

The establishment picked Charles "Trey" Grayson. The grassroots picked Rand Paul.

Not beholden to parties and institutions, grassroots Tea Party voters were able to seek out the right messengers—the men and women who would bring to Washington a real message of real change. They were free to find candidates who were more committed to cutting spending and reducing the size of government than to toeing the party line. They sought candidates who were genuinely committed to the Constitution as a blueprint for good government.

These Tea Party messengers had, and still have, the freedom to tell the truth about how the bloated public sector is robbing the private sector of its vitality. More important, they have the drive and determination to institute real change through actual budget cuts—not just reduced rates of spending. These messengers of limited government insist on serious fiscal reform measures like Cut, Cap, and Balance. They are committed to ending the destructive bailout culture and reaffirming the foundational principle that with individual liberty comes individual responsibility. The Tea Party looked for candidates who understood the only power on earth great enough to destroy America was its own federal government.

The right messengers—the men and women who will bring the message of change to Washington—are in it for their country, not for building a political career. It is refreshing how many of these new members do not care about reelection. They are coming to do real work and are refusing to be dissuaded by fear over how their boldness will affect the next campaign.

The irony, of course, is that their commitment to principle makes them more attractive candidates. And through their example, perhaps this new generation of reformers will prove honesty and integrity to be the new keys to electoral victory.

When I was elected to the U.S. House in 1998, I was sworn in with eighteen other freshman Republicans—about half of whom vowed to obey a self-imposed term limit pledge. Only three kept their pledge. I was one of them. So was Senator Pat Toomey.

Washington changes people. Candidates who boldly proclaim they will fight for change, once elected, do not withstand the crushing pressure from party leadership, constituents, interest groups, and the media. Many politicians walk through the front door of the Capitol pumped up and ready to take on the world—but walk out completely deflated.

Americans' disdain and apathy toward the political process have grown as we have watched one champion of "change" after another drink the Beltway Kool-Aid, "grow in office," and join the Washington establishment. Why, many citizens wonder, should they even bother to get involved with politics? Why vote?

Unfortunately, this consistent discouragement has created an environment in Washington in which politicians' integrity doesn't have to amount to much because voters no longer expect much. As citizens have become even more disaffected and apathetic about politics, government has become less accountable and the political establishment even more entrenched, incestuous, cynical, insulated, and corrupt.

The 2010 midterm elections shocked the establishment and blasted fresh air into the stale and dusty corridors of Washington, D.C. A wave of Tea Party–inspired Republican freshmen in the House and Senate began to open the curtains and shine some sunlight into the dark corners of the Capitol.

Finally, change had come to Washington. But had it really?

Only a few months after these new and anxious Republicans were sworn in, the musty smell of cigar smoke and stench of backroom deals seemed to return to the Capitol. In March, the government showdown over the 2011 budget ended with a deal that cut almost nothing from the budget—despite the pledge by Republicans to cut $100 billion.

And then after much nail-biting, the threat-of-default debt limit debacle concluded in August with a last-minute, behind-closed-doors grand compromise that actually allowed spending and debt to increase. Tea Party activists felt like jilted lovers, and many began to suspect that their candidates had been nothing more than the same smooth-talking politicians who had wooed them into a one-night stand.

Even worse, the Tea Party was *blamed* for the lousy deals they opposed. They were called "Tea Party Terrorists," and accused of obstructing any Republican efforts to compromise. But it was the Tea Party and conservative activists who had led the effort to compromise. Hundreds of grassroots organizations and Tea Party groups joined in support of the House Republicans' Cut, Cap, and Balance plan that did compromise in a positive way with the President—it gave him the increase in the debt limit in return for real cuts in spending, but only if Congress sent a balanced budget amendment to the states for ratification.

House Republicans passed Cut, Cap, and Balance overwhelmingly with even some Democrat support. But Democrat Majority Leader Harry Reid would not even allow the bill on the floor of the Senate for debate. The Republicans offered a compromise—and the Democrats simply tabled it. Democrats would not even consider letting states decide whether the federal government should balance its budget.

So who, exactly, was unwilling to compromise?

Conservative activists and other concerned citizens tried to be a constructive part of the debate by backing the Cut, Cap, and Balance plan that was supported by a large majority of Americans. And what did these patriots and vigilant citizens get for their trouble? They were viciously vilified and even blamed for the "Tea Party downgrade" when Standard and Poor's downgraded America's AAA credit rating.

Unbelievable. But sadly, this is how Washington operates.

## The Tea Party Did Change Washington

The debt limit deal was a big disappointment for many activists who had rallied to support Tea Party Republicans in 2010. Unfortunately, many of the newly elected freshman Republicans ultimately voted for the deal. But are all Republican politicians wedded to failure, constantly leaving Tea Party activists standing at the altar, time and again?

Absolutely not! Citizen activism in 2010 did change Washington and, I believe, changed it permanently.

This change came quickly in the Senate. In the first meeting of the Senate Republican Conference after the 2010 elections, freshman senators succeeded in accomplishing something the experts said could never happen: we passed a resolution banning pork-barrel, parochial earmarks. This had the effect of shifting power away from senior appropriators accustomed to amassing personal power and national debt by directing taxpayer money anywhere they pleased. But after the 2010 freshmen arrived, the power shifted into the hands of those who were committed to cutting spending.

The second resolution we passed was to support a balanced budget amendment to the Constitution. Nearly half the members of our conference were not happy with these changes, but they were overruled—by a new majority of commonsense conservatives focused on what was good for the nation in the long run.

For a moment, something new and amazing was happening— the American people were in charge of the U.S. Congress.

It took many elections to bring America to its current crisis, and it will take at least a few more to turn things around.

But it can be done and is already being done. The key is to elect more people who will change Washington instead of being changed by Washington. The American people must remain vigilant. Only through their dedication to holding their elected officials accountable can we continue to make real progress.

## Ideology Is Important, But Character Is Indispensable

The differences between a slick salesman and a charismatic leader are often hard to tell. I have been fooled many times myself. If you are a trusting person, as I am, it is easy to be duped by someone who is pretending to be something they are not—it happens in every profession.

Especially in politics.

Even candidates who honestly believe what they tell voters during their campaigns don't always fulfill their promises once in office. It's easy to lose your bearings when your points of reference change. While campaigning, especially if you are campaigning as a private citizen and not an incumbent, all of your points of reference are in the private sector—family, church, businesses, local media, and grassroots activists. Such candidates try to weld together the things they really believe voters want to hear. At this stage, these candidates are free to talk about what should be done—unencumbered by the often more complicated realities of actually accomplishing goals once elected.

Once in office and especially in Washington, your points of reference become the party leadership, national media, lobbyists, organized constituent groups back home, and your political opponents in both parties. For many, bold campaign promises fade, and the harsh realities of the surrounding institutional inertia consume them. Even the smallest reforms in the right direction, once considered easy and doable, suddenly become impossible . . . or at least get put off until after the next election. And the next one.

This is why most congressmen and senators simply give up on bold ideas and big reforms, and instead spend their years in office trying to bring home the bacon and supporting nice-sounding new and expensive federal programs that garner, unsurprisingly, bipartisan support. Washington politicians say to one another, "I'll support your boondoggle if you support mine." This makes them appear to be respectable, mainstream, and enlightened bipartisans, and it also makes for good press back home.

But after years of such bipartisan cooperation, Americans woke up to find their country drowning in debt, an economy paralyzed by a micromanagerial tax code, smothering regulations, a legal system that penalizes innovation and discourages risk taking. Ultimately, the aforementioned have yielded a status quo that still believes limited government and balancing the budget are radical ideas.

To save America, we must change Washington—and we will never effectively do so until we change the people we send to Washington.

This means we have to change how we select candidates.

What candidates believe and say is important. It is critical that candidates know history and have a foundational understanding of the principles that have made America great. Without this knowledge any good intentions they might have will not necessarily prevent them from doing more harm than good in the political arena. It is also important that candidates know how to translate core principles into coherent policies and legislation.

But even many Democrats seem to know the right principles, which is why they often campaign on them. They know voters respond to conservative ideas of limited government, less taxes, and more freedom. Even Barack Obama ran on these principles. He promised to cut spending and go through the budget line by line to eliminate waste. He promised to cut taxes for 95 percent of Americans. He said he would make America the best place in the world to do business.

Yes, that's what he said. But actually doing this is an entirely different matter.

In politics, ideology and rhetoric are useless unless elected leaders have character, courage, and competence. Character means having honesty and integrity. It means being committed to others and to selfless causes that are bigger than yourself. It means you are accountable to a set of principles that don't change for expedience or because of pressure. And, for me, it means being accountable to God, who judges my heart and, ultimately, my life.

Character cannot be determined by claims and promises—it is revealed over the course of one's life. Every candidate for public office will have a record of performance in their family life, their professional life, their church, their community, and volunteer activity and, if they have served in other elected offices, their voting record and behavior in office. It is important that we evaluate the character of candidates. We shouldn't expect perfection, but there is usually a discernible pattern of character in most people's lives. If a candidate has not been honest with those closest to him— his family, friends, and community—we should not be surprised if integrity is also lacking in his public life.

But although character is important, it isn't everything. There are many good people with strong personal character in elected office today, but this does not mean they will champion the cause of freedom. For some, especially most Democrats, they simply do not share the American vision of limited government, decentralized political power, and the centrality of individualism. For others, especially Republicans, they do not have the courage of their convictions. Some of the boldest conservative candidates I've seen have turned out to be some of the most cowardly congressmen and senators.

The temptation to go along with nice-sounding, bipartisan legislation is really stronger than you might think. Most average citizens recognized that the 2010 "Cash for Clunkers" program was a ridiculous idea. This was a program where the federal government paid car dealers to buy used cars and have them destroyed so people would be forced to drive more environmentally friendly new cars. In Washington, it sounded like a brilliant idea: help the environment while bailing out the ailing car industry.

But in the real world, Cash for Clunkers was a stupid idea in many ways. The federal government had to borrow the money to do it because we were already broke. Destroying used cars cost a lot of money, used a lot of energy, and reduced the supply of used cars—making these more affordable vehicles more expensive for lower-income people already hurt by the recession.

Most of the new cars that were bought by the program were imports, so it really didn't help the domestic car industry. Reports of fraud by dealers and companies that were supposed to destroy the used cars were rampant. And to top it all off, the government completely mismanaged the program, spent several billion dollars, and closed it down after a few weeks.

Still, some in Washington insisted it was a success. Why would elected leaders in Congress support such a program? Democrats supported it because they honestly believe in government management of our economy. For them it was a decision consistent with their principles. For some Republicans, however, it was just a lack of courage to say no. Car dealers from all over the nation who were big supporters of our campaigns called our offices pleading with us to support the program. They desperately needed help selling cars. Environmentalists and most of the media thought it was a brilliant idea. The U.S. Chamber of Commerce and other business groups were behind it. How could anyone not support a program that purported to help the environment, destroy old polluting cars, and save the auto industry?

The noise level inside the Capitol in support of Cash for Clunkers was deafening. It seemed the whole world supported this program. You had to be a Neanderthal to be against it. The pack mentality set in; based on the conversations in the Republican conference meeting, I thought most of our members supported it. Most did, along with practically every Democrat.

And what did it all amount to? Another $3 billion down the drain.

I voted against it along with a few dozen Republicans. Voting no may seem like a small thing, but it wasn't. Some of my best friends and biggest campaign supporters are car dealers. I also voted against business groups that were usually my allies in fights to create jobs and a better economy. And I was portrayed in the media as an anti-environmental right-wing nut.

There are dozens of equally stupid and equally supported programs like this offered in Congress each year. Every time I vote no, I alienate friends, allies, and campaign supporters. Few members of Congress are willing to take this kind of pain and rejection year after year. I have been called "Senator No" because there are very few bills that come through Congress that actually deserve a yes vote.

It takes courage and a thick skin to continually say no to all the boneheaded ideas that come through Congress. For me, that courage is fueled by support from a few conservative colleagues and millions of Americans who are pleading with us to keep fighting. These Americans see the big picture, and that is why loud and vocal citizen activism is so important. We've got to counter the yes noise inside of Washington with even louder "no way" demands from the American people. Your voice is the only antidote for D.C. corruption, so when the American people remain silent, Washington wins.

Courage can be contagious—but only if citizens encourage it.

Competence is another often-overlooked attribute of candidates. If a candidate has not accomplished anything of significance in the real world, it is unlikely he or she will accomplish much as an elected leader. President Obama is a good example, as his entire career is mostly based on delivering speeches. Accomplished and competent candidates are not always the best salesmen. Voters will need to decide whether they want a showman or a leader, and these attributes are rarely in the same package.

## How to Choose the Candidates with Character, Courage, and Competence

When voters pick a candidate, they are choosing someone to speak for them—a messenger to tell the government what it should and should not do. Choosing the right candidates to be our messengers—those who understand the principles of American exceptionalism and have the character, courage, and competence to represent their fellow citizens effectively—is difficult.

I certainly don't have a perfect record picking candidates, but I've learned a lot about how to select good people who are worth the effort. When I was a private citizen and uninvolved with politics, I picked candidates based on friendships, referrals, or arbitrary criteria such as, "He seems like a good guy." I believe many voters think about politics this way. Also, what the government did twenty years ago didn't seem as intrusive and threatening to me as it does today, so I didn't give much thought to the peculiar people who ran for office. But, then again, I really didn't expect them to do much if they were elected, anyway. Yet, apparently they were expanding government, borrowing money, and creating a lot of debt while I wasn't paying attention!

After I was elected to Congress, my endorsements were based more on a candidate's ability to articulate a conservative agenda. The smart ones memorized my priorities from my campaign brochures or my website, and then recited my positions back to me. I thought they were brilliant, but this approach to picking the right candidates had mixed results.

After years of frustration with politicians who demonstrated little character, courage, or competence in office, I started the Senate Conservatives Fund to support candidates who would help me save America. By 2008, I was desperate. So was the nation.

Five of the candidates I supported through the Senate Conservatives Fund in 2010 were elected to the Senate, and they have proven to be individuals who are true to their principles and unafraid to take stands against bad legislation. Here's how we knew they would be strong, commonsense senators before we endorsed them:

## Pat Toomey (Pennsylvania)

Pat and I were elected to the U.S. House of Representatives in 1998. He was a successful businessman who graduated from Harvard. This displays competence. I knew him as a man of great personal integrity who possessed the courage to stand up to both big-spending Democrats and big-spending Republicans. His voting record was consistently conservative even though he represented a swing district with a strong union presence. That took courage.

Pat kept his voluntary term limit pledge and left the House after six years (integrity). He ran against sitting Republican senator Arlen Specter, who was supported by President George W. Bush and the entire Republican establishment even though Specter voted against the GOP more than he voted with us. Toomey came within a percentage point of beating Specter in that primary. Again, competence.

After losing to Specter, Toomey became president of the Club for Growth and began to campaign against RINOs (Republicans In Name Only). Six years later, he announced he was running against Specter again. This time, Specter saw he couldn't beat Toomey as a Republican, so he became a Democrat. He lost the race, anyway.

Toomey is a dedicated family man, a pilot, a businessman, and now a commonsense conservative senator. The people of Pennsylvania recognized him as a principled candidate with character, courage, and competence.

## Marco Rubio (Florida)

Rubio's parents were Cuban refugees who came to America with nothing. They worked hard and managed to get Marco through law school. He became a successful attorney. By the time he was in his mid-thirties, he was Speaker of the Florida House of Representatives, where he established a record of integrity and accomplishment. This shows competence.

After serving as Speaker, Rubio had a clear path to become Florida's attorney general, but he could see that America was in trouble. Marco decided to run for the U.S. Senate in a Republican primary against a popular sitting Republican governor, Charlie Crist, who was supported by the entire Republican establishment in both Florida and Washington (courage).

Rubio mounted a successful Senate campaign by inspiring Floridians and Americans throughout the country with his message of freedom and opportunity, by demonstrating the qualifications of a great representative—before he was elected.


## Rand Paul (Kentucky)

A dedicated family man, community volunteer, and physician who had never run for public office, Rand Paul had lived a life of character, courage, and competence before entering politics.

It took a lot of courage to run for the U.S. Senate against an opponent who was supported by the Republican leader in the Senate and most sitting GOP senators. Yet, despite never having run for public office, Rand organized an effective campaign and won his race against overwhelming odds.

Like his father, Rand's lifelong belief in the principles of freedom and individual liberty have defined his philosophy and shaped his politics. Much like my own relationship with the Tea Party, this grassroots movement gave Paul the opportunity to help harness a popular passion for fixing this country and take that message to Washington, D.C. Within a few months after becoming a U.S. senator, Paul quickly established his national reputation as a strong conservative leader with character, courage, and competence.

## Mike Lee (Utah)

Lee is a dedicated family man and successful attorney. He is a constitutional scholar who clerked for Supreme Court Justice Samuel Alito (competence).

At thirty-nine years old, Lee decided to take on sitting Republican senator Bob Bennett, a senior appropriator who was a member of the Republican leadership. Bennett was a strong proponent of earmarks and actively worked to kill any effort to stop parochial, pork-barrel spending. Bennett was supported in his reelection effort by the entire Washington establishment.

Mike Lee demonstrated real courage by challenging a senior sitting Republican senator. Lee stood on the conservative principles of limited constitutional government and went after the big-spending earmark proponents in Washington. He had demonstrated character and competence in his personal life, and when he took on the entire Washington establishment, I knew he had the courage to stand for freedom.

## Ron Johnson (Wisconsin)

Wisconsin is often considered the center of progressive liberalism in America. Over the decades, voters in that state have sent some of the most liberal Democrat congressmen and senators to Washington.

Ron Johnson, a businessman and self-made millionaire who had never run for public office, decided to leave his business and take on Democratic senator Russ Feingold. Johnson was willing to spend millions of his own money in a long-shot effort to replace the liberal Feingold.

Johnson ran on a commitment to make government smaller and more accountable. Ron was told he had no chance of winning, yet he was willing to risk everything he had worked for to try to save his country. He had demonstrated character and competence in all areas of his life, and his willingness to face the long odds in his senate race proved he had the courage to change Washington.

## What Candidates Say Versus What They Do

After gauging whether or not particular candidates have the character, courage, and competence to make a positive difference in Washington, I try to make sure their policy positions are consistent with their stated principles. The Senate Conservatives Fund has developed a questionnaire that we require candidates to complete before we consider an endorsement.

Again, I am not looking for perfection, and I don't expect candidates that I support to always agree with me. I am not always right. There are many votes and positions on issues where honest, thinking people can disagree. But a candidate's answers to these questions will reveal whether they consistently apply conservative principles to their positions on important issues.

## *Questions the Senate Conservatives Fund Asks Candidates*

Many candidates don't like to fill out questionnaires or sign pledges. This locks them into specific positions on issues. But this is precisely our intent with the questionnaire for the Senate Conservatives Fund (P.O. Box 388, Alexandria, VA 22313, (877) 838-9388). If candidates are not willing to commit to specific positions on issues before they are elected, there is little chance they will stand firm on anything after they are elected.

Some Republicans have suggested that we should not emphasize social and moral issues. I agree that government should not promote religion or moral opinions. But government should not expunge moral values from our culture or promote behavior that is costly and destructive to society as a whole.

When government sanctions behavior by paying for it or by legalizing activity that is costly and destructive to society as a whole, citizens must hold government and lawmakers accountable. The issue of abortion will expose a candidate's views about the dignity of life and the importance of the individual. The issue of taxpayer-funded abortion will reveal if a candidate is willing to allow the government to violate the conscience of people by making them pay for abortions when they are morally opposed to the procedure.

It is rare to find a congressman or senator who is both pro-abortion and supportive of individual liberty. Most proabortion politicians are for big government, central economic planning, and collectivist social policies because they do not believe in the dignity of the individual. This is not universally true. There are some fiscal conservatives and libertarians who support abortion, but I have found these politicians are often inconsistent and unprincipled in their approach to federal policy.

Questions #1 and #2 on the SCF questionnaire asks the following questions about abortion (candidates are asked to answer yes, no, or undecided, and space is provided for brief explanatory comments):

1. Will you oppose taxpayer funding for any organization that provides abortions or that funds organizations that provide abortions, including Planned Parenthood?

2. Will you support legislation recognizing the personhood of the unborn child?

The definition of marriage is also a key question to determine how candidates view the role of government. Does government have the right to reshape cultural mores by redefining religious institutions to sanction behavior that is considered immoral by all the world's religions? In America, people should have a right to live with whomever they want, but redefining marriage to promote behavior that is deemed to be costly and destructive by the Centers for Disease Control is not the proper role of the government. Question #3 tells us where candidates stand on marriage and the role of government on other issues as well.

3. Do you believe that marriage should be legally defined as between one man and one woman, and do you oppose government-sanctioned civil unions and domestic partnerships?

The Second Amendment is about a lot more than guns. It tells us if a candidate takes the Constitution seriously. Question #4 is simple and to the point:

> 4. Do you agree that the Second Amendment to the U.S. Constitution guarantees an individual the right to keep and bear arms, and will you oppose all measures that infringe on this right?

Taxes reveal a lot about a candidate. Nearly half of all Americans pay no federal income taxes, and the Democrats want to expand this number by shifting more of the tax burden to the top 3 percent—the same people who create most of the jobs in America and already pay more than 50 percent of all income taxes. Questions #5, #6, and #7 tell us where candidates stand on taxes.

> 5. Will you oppose all net tax increases?
> 6. Will you support fundamental tax reform that replaces the IRS tax code with a low single-rate system that makes it easier for Americans to accumulate wealth?
> 7. Will you support the full, complete, and permanent repeal of the death tax?

The issue of earmarks reveals if a candidate understands that congressmen and senators are not elected to promote parochial interests. Our job is to do what's best for the United States of America. Candidates who think their job is to bring home the bacon will likely focus more on hometown "attaboys" than protecting and defending the Constitution. Question #8 is designed to get candidates on record about keeping the ban on earmarks:

8. Do you agree that earmarks encourage wasteful spending and lead to corruption, and will you abstain from requesting earmarks, vote against all earmarks, and work to reform the federal spending process so taxpayer funds are allocated according to a competitive or formula-based system?

The most important issue for the 2012 elections will be the passage of a constitutional amendment to balance the federal budget. Without it, we will bankrupt America. Question #9 advocates for a specific form of a balanced budget amendment.

9. Will you support an amendment to the U.S. Constitution that would force Congress to balance the federal budget, prohibit federal spending from exceeding 18 percent of GDP, and require a two-thirds super-majority to raise taxes?

Repealing ObamaCare is also essential to saving our healthcare system and balancing our budget.

10. Will you support the complete repeal of Obama-Care?

Questions #11 through #19 query candidates on a wide range of issues.

11. Do you agree that government bailouts of private companies undermine our free market system by rewarding failure and punishing success, and will you pledge to oppose all bailouts?

12. Will you support efforts to reform Social Security by transitioning younger workers into a system built upon their personal savings, which cannot be raided by politicians in Washington?

13. Do you agree that a secure and reliable energy supply for Americans requires a strong and dynamic energy market, free from government distortions (including subsidies, tariffs, price controls, and unnecessary regulations)?

14. Do you believe that lawsuit abuse is harming American businesses, consumers, and families, and will you support legal reforms such as a loser-pays system that makes those who file unsuccessful lawsuits liable for the defendant's legal bills?

15. Do you believe education decisions are best made at the local level, and will you support efforts to allow states to opt out of the federal No Child Left Behind law?

16. Do you oppose amnesty for illegal immigrants, and do you agree our borders must be secured and our immigration laws must be enforced?

17. Will you support the National Right to Work Act, which protects workers from being forced to join a union as a condition of employment?

18. Do you believe that the role of a Supreme Court Justice is to narrowly interpret the law based on the writ-

ten text of the Constitution, and will you pledge to only vote to confirm Supreme Court nominees who share this philosophy?

19. Will you support an amendment to the U.S. Constitution limiting the time someone can serve in Congress to three terms in the House and two terms in the Senate?

Questions #20 through #22 allow candidates to write in their thoughts and qualify their answers.

20. Why are you running for the U.S. Senate?

21. Please list any policy positions that differ from conservative beliefs.

22. Please list the five individuals who currently hold elective office that you most admire. (Do not include Jim DeMint.)

## Share the Truth

- Candidates who don't keep their promises have discouraged voters and created widespread citizen apathy about politics.
- When voters are disengaged and apathetic, government becomes unaccountable and corrupt.
- To change Washington we have to change the people who are there. This means changing the way we select candidates.
- Candidates must understand and be committed to the principles of American exceptionalism.

- Candidates must have a history of demonstrating character, courage, and competence in their lives prior to running for public office.
- Find out where candidates stand on important issues before you support them. Make sure they are committed to conservative principles and policies.

# 9

# What You Can Do to Save America

## Introduction by Grass-Roots Activist Dave Zupan

French political thinker Alexis de Tocqueville once observed: "The greatness of America lies not in being more enlightened than any other nation, but rather in her ability to *repair* her *faults*."

Taking our cue from de Tocqueville's observation, if we expect our liberties to remain intact, we must be, in a sense, repairmen. But to repair our country, we must first show up for the job.

Showing up can be both the easiest and hardest part. I "showed up" in the political world by becoming involved in my first campaign after a friend suggested I help out, handing out literature and talking with voters. This was my first step, but there are other things you can do, like attending city council or school board meetings, for instance. Showing up at such meetings doesn't mean you need to speak, at least not at first. If you are simply present at a few city council meetings, like I was, people will become curious. Curious about why you keep coming, perhaps even wondering if you're considering running for office—which is exactly what I asked on just my third visit to my local city council.

Once you become familiar with the process, you will want to speak up at city council meetings. After I got comfortable going to meetings, I began pressing my city council officials about how they were going to spend tax dollars. Because a handful of people were going to these meetings and were paying attention, we were able to stop raises for our city mayor and nonbargaining city employees. We also blocked unnecessary funding for regional transit—just by raising our concerns at these meetings.

Chances are there is an active Tea Party group in your area. Usually, there are speakers at these meetings who will help you understand how local, state, and federal government operates. Elected officials will often speak. Try going to a meeting to learn about the group's mission and consider joining.

In years past during each election, I would simply write a check to the party and candidate I thought best represented my views. I would just vote in every election and consider my duty was done. I would then hit the snooze button on my political alarm clock thinking my elected representatives would generally do what they promised during the campaign.

But the alarm that woke me up, and millions of other Americans during the 2008 election cycle, was when we realized what was happening to our republic—"stimulus," bailouts, TARP, more government, more collectivism, and more debt. Like millions of Americans, I realized that I had been sleeping on the job. There is more to a citizen's duty than simply writing checks to parties or candidates, and even more than just voting. We must begin to monitor our elected officials. We must keep an eye on government leaders at every level.

And we can do this best by standing tall, speaking out, and showing up.

At forty years old, my wife and I had four children, a small business from which we were barely eking out a living, a dozen employees, and a weekly schedule packed with volunteer work in our church and community. When it came to politics, I was the stereotypical uninvolved, uninformed American citizen— I was simply way too busy for any of that nonsense. I thought that government was an expensive nuisance, but it seemed to be on autopilot and out of my control.

I always considered voting to be my civic duty, but I was generally uninformed about the candidates and the issues, and I really had no interest in ever being directly involved in politics. I had never darkened the door of any Republican Party functions or attended our local precinct organizational meetings. In my opinion, politicians were sort of like grown-up hall monitors from high school who just wanted to run everyone's lives.

And I was having a hard enough time trying to run my own life.

The reason I mention this is because I cannot condemn anyone who doesn't have the time or inclination to be involved with politics. But here's the rub: our nation's crushing debt and collapsing economy are not only my problems—they are my fault. Showing up every two to four years is important—but I did not include political vigilance as part of my civic responsibilities.

The U.S. Constitution is a legal contract that conveys the important fact that control of our government and nation belongs to its citizens. The federal government is, by law, a government of the people, by the people, and for the people. This is not simply an offer that citizens can or should ignore; it is a birthright we must cherish.

And it is a responsibility that involves much more than just voting.

How did I go from an uninvolved and relatively apathetic citizen to a U.S. senator? My interest in politics really began to develop when a candidate for Congress asked me to help with his campaign. My business background was marketing and strategic planning—and this unknown and underfunded candidate wanted my expertise in developing a communications and organizational campaign plan.

But he wanted me to do it for free!

Nevertheless, I was a sucker for a worthy cause and his "throw the bums out" philosophy seemed like something worth fighting for. Soon enough, I had added "campaign strategy development" to my long list of volunteer activities.

That's when I began to learn about politics.

As I learned more about government, elections, and politics, I began to connect the dots between politics and the issues that were affecting my family and my community. Perverse incentives from federal welfare programs were encouraging a pathology of government dependence, destroying marriages and families, leading to more high school dropouts, more crime, and increased poverty. The majority of the volunteer work I was doing to help our community was dealing with problems caused directly or indirectly by bad government policies.

I also began to realize that federal education mandates had turned our schools into politically correct day care centers—where everything that is good about America was bad, and vice versa. The tax, regulatory, and legal systems designed by politicians that had little to no private sector experience were making it harder for businesses like mine to succeed. The more informed and involved I became, the more I saw how politics impacted every area of my life and the lives of my fellow citizens, the more interested I became in changing things. I began to think that we could make America work a lot more effectively if we just elected better politicians.

When my candidate for Congress won an upset victory in 1992 over a popular incumbent congresswoman, my eyes were opened to the possibilities of citizen involvement in politics. We had organized a motley crew of political novices, held countless small group meetings across the district, knocked on thousands of doors, and won a stunning victory that was called one of the biggest political upsets in South Carolina history. And we did it with almost no money!

By helping just this one candidate, I had learned a lot about how on-the-ground politics works. During his campaign, I went to many Republican gatherings in the district. I learned how to organize volunteers to make calls and leave door hangers on thousands of homes. I wrote campaign brochures, videos, and opinion editorials. I also learned how to raise money.

When the new congressman stepped down six years later to run for the U.S. Senate, I decided to try my hand as a candidate. In 1998, I was elected to the U.S. House of Representatives. Six years later, I was elected to the U.S. Senate.

Politics is not rocket science. It's common sense. Much of what I did in my business and as a community volunteer transferred easily into the political arena. Politics, like marketing, is all about ideas and people. It's about inspiring, persuading, and meeting people's needs. It's about solving problems and beating the competition.

But I also learned that politics was about things that are much bigger than my little corner of the world in Greenville, South Carolina. Politics in the United States often decides the future of the world, determining whether my children and grandchildren will enjoy freedom and prosperity, and also determining whether there will even be an American future worth having. Politics creates the framework that guides our fate. And as often as we justifiably resent the process, politics provides citizens the opportunity to construct a framework that preserves the American Dream.

My involvement with one political campaign ignited my love for America and for freedom. It showed me how I could become a more vigilant citizen. But you don't have to run for office to make a difference. In fact, there are many citizens who have a far greater and more enduring influence on the future of America than those on Capitol Hill.

That's because it has always been the private sector that has made America great. People who raise families, work, volunteer in their communities, and who are informed voters: they are the freedom-loving individuals who make America work. The more active these citizens are in electing good representatives, the stronger our nation will be in the future.

## We Must Understand the Role of Government

Vigilant citizens should know how our government works, but even more important, they must know what government is supposed to do. Citizens who simply assume the role of government is to do good things will more likely become part of the problem than part of the solution.

When I was a volunteer leader for the United Way, my job was to do good things for people in need. We raised as much money as possible and helped as many people as we could with the often limited resources we received. When I was a deacon in my church, my job was to help families in need. When I volunteered in my children's schools, my job was to help create a better education environment. As the CEO of my small company, my job was to make a profit and grow the business.

Wherever I worked, I tried to do good things.

As an official of the federal government, my job is very different. I took an oath to protect and defend a Constitution that limits what the federal government can do, and the explicit functions of the federal government are found in Article I, Section 8. The Founders intended for the powers of the federal government to be specific and limited. The federal government is supposed to defend the nation, regulate commerce between the states, provide for national roads ("postal roads") and harbors, maintain a sound currency, protect private property rights, and promote justice. There are few other things the federal government should be doing—and our Founders limited its role precisely because they knew centralized power yields corruption.

Of course, many who want to use the government to do good have honorable intentions. However, it is not my job as a U.S. senator to think of good things to do. It is not my job or that of the government to go out and survey America, discover problems, and use taxpayer dollars to attempt to solve them all. My job is to keep the government focused on its specific constitutional responsibilities and leave the rest to the states and the people.

The primary function of Congress is to write laws that allow for a free society. The executive branch is supposed to make sure these laws are implemented and equally applied to all citizens. Federal laws should protect individual rights and private property, encourage a robust free market economy, and ensure justice.

It is simply not our job to do good deeds and solve every problem.

The federal government should write the rules and serve as referees. It is not our role to be the coaches, players, or fans. Yet, this is exactly what our modern government tries to do. The federal government is attempting to micromanage banks, businesses, schools, physicians, and hospitals, the energy industry, the auto industry, the housing industry, the financial markets, and just about everything that moves in America.

Worst of all, because those of us in Washington are so distracted trying to centrally manage every aspect of the nation, we are not effectively carrying out our constitutional responsibilities. Wasteful spending on nonfederal functions has created debt that now threatens our ability to defend the nation. The Federal

Reserve has done everything imaginable but help to create a sound monetary system. Interstate commerce, as well as our ability to compete globally, is severely impeded by an antiquated and unnecessarily complicated tax system, burdensome regulations, and frivolous lawsuits.

The very nature of bureaucracy dictates that effective management cannot be accomplished through a political structure. Quality and efficiency are achieved best through decentralized organizations and professional managers. History, experience, and common sense have proven that the federal government cannot manage our education, health-care, financial, energy, and transportation systems from Washington, D.C.

The reason the Founders insisted on a written charter like our Constitution to limit the role of the federal government was precisely to avoid the dysfunction and debt that now threaten our survival. There is a big difference in the practical roles of organizations like the United Way and a country like the United States. Citizens who do not understand this difference should continue as community volunteers—but they should stay out of politics.

## Be an Informed Citizen

Being an informed citizen requires more than just vague awareness of the problems we face as a nation. It begins with understanding the competing visions between the two political parties as discussed in chapter 4.

The differences between the Democratic and Republican parties at the national level are irreconcilable. Constant compromise between the two parties has created a floundering national economy and an unsustainable national debt. Critics continue to demand cooperation and bipartisanship, but informed voters must understand that the massive expansion of the federal government and our debt over the past decade is a direct result of bipartisanship.

There simply can be no positive compromise between freedom and socialism, between centralized economic planning and decentralized free markets; between collectivism and individualism. In Washington, bipartisan compromise has never resulted in spending cuts, the elimination of wasteful programs, or reductions of regulations. It may mean a smaller increase in spending, fewer new wasteful programs, and slightly less onerous regulations—but it has always meant more spending and bigger government.

Democrats will never agree to real reductions in the size and scope of the federal government. They will not agree to the elimination of duplicative federal programs without tax increases or additional spending in other areas. They will not agree to help people escape from government dependency with individualistic reforms of Social Security and Medicare. Nor will they devolve the functions of education and health care to the states. A Washington Democrat's worldview is so federally focused that he will lead you to believe that if he isn't in charge of something, it simply ceases to exist.

That said, not all Democrats at local and state levels share the same philosophy as Democrats in Washington. But Democrats at the federal level, especially Senate Democrats, simply cannot be elected unless they march to the tune of the big labor unions, radical environmentalists, and collectivist-minded special interests. Democrats at this level derive all of their political power from a heavily centralized government power—and bigger government and more union workers mean more dependent voters.

Democrats have no interest in changing the status quo because their power depends on maintaining it.

Too often, when Republicans compromise with Democrats, America loses. We must stop their agenda or at least slow them down until we can defeat them, but make no mistake—we have to defeat them in order to save this country.

Democrats have grown their power by increasing the number of government dependents, expanding the number of unionized government workers, and convincing Americans that they will help the poor and the middle class. If only this were true.

The Democrats' economic policies are destroying jobs and prosperity because Democrats honestly believe that government spending grows the economy more effectively than private sector spending. This view ignores one of the most pivotal foundational principles of free market economics: markets allocate resources better than government.

Needless to say, Democrats do not believe this basic principle upon which freedom depends.

I realize this sounds harshly partisan, but the reality at hand has nothing to do with politics. This is about common sense and proven economic principles. You can't just listen to what Democrats say in order to know what they really believe. You have to look at what they do. When the Democrats had complete control of the government between 2008 and 2010, all of the programs they rammed down the throats of the American people were big-government, collectivist economics:

- nearly a trillion dollars of government spending to stimulate the economy (it sedated the economy: unemployment increased and the economy did not rebound)
- government takeover of health care with ObamaCare (the cost of health care increased immediately, and the unions who supported it are now asking for waivers)
- government takeover of banks and the financial markets with Dodd-Frank legislation (which did not even address the cause of the financial crisis—Fannie Mae and Freddie Mac)
- multiple housing and mortgage bailouts
- government takeover of General Motors and Chrysler
- expansion of government control of the energy industry

This list could be much longer, but you get the point. When in power, Democrats always expand government and spending. Republicans have had their lapses—some big ones—but nothing like the radicalism we've seen from President Obama's Democratic Party.

The Republican Party is not perfect, but its principles and platform are still generally consistent with the values of American prosperity and exceptionalism. Republicans now have the opportunity to create a large tent of disaffected Americans who have previously not been active in politics, as well as libertarians, frustrated Democrats, constitutional conservatives, and even recovering liberals.

We must now build a new Republican Party that reflects the conservative principles of decentralized federal power, free market economics, and individual responsibility. There is plenty of room for debate about how to develop policies that reflect these principles, but most important, the debate can no longer be about how much to grow the federal government.

Republicans must appeal to all working, thinking, and tax-paying Americans. This is the GOP's natural constituency, and we should encourage them to join us. Every citizen who believes in freedom and opportunity should abandon the Democratic Party and help us restore a Republican Party that is principled, passionate, and worthy of the trust of freedom-loving Americans.

Restoring the Republican Party means getting behind the right candidates in order to challenge the same old big-spending, big-government Republicans in the primaries. We must recruit principled and accomplished businesspeople, a broad and diverse cross-section of Americans—to join this fight for freedom, opportunity, and prosperity.

Frustration with both major political parties may tempt some to join a third party or to remain independent. Unfortunately, this will only help the Democrats succeed with their big-government agenda. Nearly half of Americans are dependent on the government or want even more from government. They will almost always vote for Democrats. Unless freedom-loving Americans can unite within the Republican Party, the Democrats will win every election and continue to shamelessly lead our nation toward an economic collapse, blaming everyone but themselves along the way.

## Finding Your Role as an Active Citizen

Being an active and vigilant citizen does not mean you have to spend a lot of time at Republican Party meetings or political gatherings. These activities can be beneficial for many, but there are other ways to keep government accountable.

Most businesses are part of state or national industry associations that have political action committees (PACs). These committees advocate positions with state and federal elected officials that will benefit their industry and their workers. Employers often invite rank-and-file employees to be part of their PAC leadership team. Consider volunteering to be a part of these teams.

Study the political positions advocated by your employer or their industry PAC. Too many businesses like to play both sides by supporting candidates in both parties in hopes of maintaining a good relationship with whoever wins. This corporatist approach hurts America because it does not keep candidates accountable or consistently promote progrowth economic principles.

You can be sure that labor unions do not play both sides. They punish any candidates who do not support their positions. This keeps Democrats accountable to union demands and constantly pressures Republicans to support union positions. But few businesses play hardball like the unions. For this reason Democrats vote for pro-union positions and against free market economic principles, yet still garner the support of many business groups—and all at the expense of average American workers.

American businesses are the only counterbalance to the organized political power of labor unions, radical environmentalists, trial lawyers, and other special interests. When businesses abandon progrowth principles to win the favor of Democrats, this hurts the cause of freedom. Active employees can, and should, pressure their employers to play a more constructive role in politics.

Another way to become informed and active in shaping our

government is to organize on your own. I have met with numerous small groups of business owners and managers who get together to discuss government policies and to advocate with elected leaders for better government. Some of these groups interview candidates and raise campaign money for those who win their trust.

Neighbors, members of civic groups, and fellow church members also form small groups to become involved in politics. These groups help their members become more informed and make political involvement more social and fun. It is much easier and more enjoyable to go to a political meeting, Tea Party rally, or congressman's office if you go with a group of friends with common interests.

But while being a part of a group gives movements a better critical mass, there is still plenty you can do as an individual. Telephone calls, letters, and e-mails to congressmen and senators are good ways to let them know what you think. It doesn't take a lot of calls or e-mails to my office to get my attention. Every day, I get a report of how many people contacted my office and what was on their minds. If one hundred people call about an issue, I know it's important. If one thousand people contact me, I know it's a movement—and I'd better take action.

It's easy to find contact information for congressmen and senators. A web search for "U.S. Capitol Switchboard" will bring up several sources of e-mail addresses and phone numbers. And don't limit yourself to representatives from your state. About half of my calls and e-mails come from outside of South Carolina—and it is always very helpful for me to know what Americans from all over the country are thinking.

I would also encourage you to look for opportunities just to show up. The media has tried to malign Tea Party rallies, but such shows of force by citizens can make politicians either shake in their boots or celebrate—depending on whether or not the participants at the rally are on their side. Public demonstrations keep the political process more accountable, and they have often changed the outcomes of elections, similar to what we saw in 2010.

If you have a computer and access to the Internet, you can find all the resources you need to be an active, vigilant citizen. You can find the top conservative grassroots groups in your area. Most local Tea Party groups have websites. You can find the times and stations for local and nationally syndicated radio talk shows and the best blogs to get your news.

If you have a particular issue of interest such as education, a web search of "school choice advocates" or "America's best charter schools" will give you plenty of ideas about how to get involved. But you should also watch out for groups that advocate for more government control and spending to support particular issues. We need real solutions—which naturally means looking for better ways to do things with less government.

You'll find your best role in politics just by getting started. Don't make it a full-time job. Just do a web search in an area of interest and make a call or two. Try to do something small every week, like sending an e-mail to a congressman or senator. If you find good candidates, support them the best you can. And if you want to help me elect conservative senators, you can go to SenateConservatives.com.

And, of course, you should vote. Make a commitment to take two or three people with you when you do so. Talk about voting several months before the election to remind people to register to vote. You would be amazed at how many intelligent Americans are not even registered to vote (only about 30 percent of citizens over eighteen even voted in the last election).

What can you do to save America? Get informed. Get active. And remember—there are hundreds of small things you can do that will make a big difference.

## Share the Truth

- Vigilant citizens keep the federal government accountable and responsive.
- If you're not active in politics, America's problems are not only your problems, they are your fault.
- The role of the federal government is not to solve all of our problems, but to provide a framework of laws and justice that allow freedom to work.
- The differences between the Democratic and Republican Parties are irreconcilable: there can be no compromise between collectivism and freedom.
- There are many ways to get active in politics, and getting involved in small ways will make a big difference.
- Vote and take others with you!

# 10

# It's Now or Never:
# Final Challenge

Those who expect to reap the blessings of freedom must, like men, undergo the fatigue of supporting it.

—*Thomas Paine*

N ow that I have hopefully convinced you and many other patriotic and thoughtful Americans to get involved with the political process, I have a confession: I hate politics. Being involved with politics has been, without a doubt, the most unnatural, unseemly, irrational, and frustrating venture of my entire life. It has literally been mind-numbing to deal with the astounding ignorance and laziness of the media, endless self-serving politicians, and far too many citizens dependent on government. Almost everyone in politics always seems to be twisting or ignoring the facts. Dishonesty is as blatant as it is rampant. Lying is more often the norm than the exception.

Freedom is a messy business. Welcome to the fight!

Good, decent, and honest people understandably do not like to be involved in such nastiness. That's why so many have often left the operation of government to those who are not good, decent, or honest. But the real problem is not simply bad people in politics, but "good" people who are willing to ignore facts and common sense in order to do "good" things with other people's money. These people are dangerous precisely because they can justify any means to achieve what they imagine to be righteous goals. Most everyday Americans don't have the kind of money it takes to jump into politics, and yet Washington elites shamelessly take as much as they can from taxpayers to redistribute as they see fit.

I entered the political world as a mild-mannered and peace-loving Christian businessman who always tried to avoid conflict. But in Washington, I have constantly and consistently had my civility tested to the point of losing it. As I continue to watch my country's journey toward destruction, I fear I've reached the breaking point. I am fed up with being fed up. By always being outraged, I am now outraged out. I have been forced to voice harsh criticisms of others—often being downright unfriendly and unkind—but even my harshest statements are usually, quite frankly, gross understatements of the even harsher truth. To constantly bite one's tongue in politics would be to completely bite it off. Voters sent me to Washington to fight for them and our country, and to tell the truth, however difficult it might be.

We are mindlessly destroying the world's last bastion of freedom and hope. We are carelessly frittering away humanity's greatest achievement—a nation where even the lowest among us has the opportunity to use their God-given talents to achieve dreams unimaginable anywhere else in the world. We are needlessly turning our backs on a precious gift handed down to us by men and women who sacrificed their lives, their treasures, and their sacred honor. Ronald Reagan's shining city on a hill grows ever dimmer. America's future becomes dangerously dark.

For telling the truth, I have been called a conservative firebrand. Those who know me would not describe me as being full of fire, but admittedly, my rhetoric at times has been heated. On a radio interview in the summer of 2011, I said bluntly that Barack Obama was the most antibusiness and anti-American president of my lifetime. Sometimes I cringe to think that I actually said that about an American president. But I believe my statement was true and needed to be said. It still needs to be said, and often.

America's economic foundation has always relied on individuals who take financial risks in return for anticipated financial rewards. Our economy works when millions of Americans take such risks, thus producing profits, better jobs, and other financial benefits. Such success encourages others to take risks—to invest, work, pursue higher education, change jobs, innovate, start businesses, and hire workers—in short, to increase their own rewards. I know this sounds simple, but few in Washington seem to grasp these elementary economic principles.

When the federal and state governments create a predictable framework of laws and regulations that incentivize venture capitalism and allow individuals to keep the rewards of their risk taking, America's free market economy thrives. But President Obama and the Democrats have done the complete opposite. They have increased the risks of doing business while reducing the rewards—and they don't seem to understand why the economy is not growing, jobs are not being produced, and America remains financially stagnant. The definition of *insanity* is to keep doing the same thing expecting different results, and the Democratic Party's economic agenda is perhaps the best current example of that definition.

President Obama's nearly $1 trillion in stimulus spending

did not reduce risks or increase rewards for the individuals that make our economy grow. Instead, the president simply gave federal money to states to help them maintain certain ineffective services and those services' bloated payrolls. Some of the money even went to bail out underfunded pension plans for government workers. The basic premise of so-called stimulus spending—pumping more money into places where it was already being squandered—meant the President's plan was destined to fail from the beginning. Obama and his party's solutions will not work precisely because they don't understand how the American economy works.

Under Obama, the risks for individual businesspeople have grown because his administration has created more uncertainty about the availability of credit, the increased cost of health care, the increased costs of unemployment insurance, the increased costs of regulations, the increased costs of energy, the increased cost of litigation, and an increased threat of unionization. In addition to increasing all of these risks, President Obama has reduced anticipated rewards by promising to increase taxes.

True to Democratic form, President Obama continues to stigmatize success by speaking of "the rich"—those who take risks and receive rewards—in derogatory ways. This President has fomented class envy by repeatedly claiming that those who make over $200,000 a year—the 3 percent of Americans who pay over half of all the taxes and create most of the jobs—do not pay their fair share of taxes. He has criticized business conventions and trade shows that promote commerce. He has condemned business aviation that allows management, customers, and suppliers to efficiently access production facilities in rural America. He has constantly carped at "big oil" and utilities that provide the energy for every American job and household. And these are just a few items.

I meant what I said, however harsh it might have sounded: President Obama *is* antibusiness.

President Obama's policies are also anti-American. This is not an accusation I make lightly. But everything this President has proposed or passed through Congress continues to routinely transfer power and money away from individuals and the states and place more of both in the hands of Washington politicians. The President is disdainful of individual decision making, the hallmark of a free society, yet lauds collectivist policies that create one-size-fits-all solutions. He has effectively socialized American health care and nationalized our banking system. He has expanded federal control of America's energy resources. He has attempted to expand the power of national labor unions at the expense of small businesses—the very people who create the majority of the jobs we so desperately need. Needless to say, this is not the American way.

And needless to say—it is not working!

This is not simply an ideological battle, some academic exercise, another partisan debate, or just another election—this is literally a make-or-break point in American history, a very real dollars-and-cents, balance-sheet time bomb that is going to explode in our faces if we don't make the right decisions now.

We may not get another opportunity. This could be our last chance. It is now or never that we decide if we are going to continue the American Dream. I am appealing to every freedom-loving American to leave your comfort zone and join this fight. As Matthew Spalding of the Heritage Foundation writes:

Our self-reliant individualists must become public-spirited citizens. Democracy requires a concern for the common good, and an initiative for advancing it, to be diffused throughout the populace.[1]

Getting involved with politics can be messy and unpleasant. But if the citizens who make America work continue to just mind their own business, protect first their dignity, profess enlightened nonpartisanship, or look down their noses at those of us who appear to be mud wrestling in public, we will lose everything that generations of Americans have fought to give us. Those who understand what's truly at stake must join this fight. The other side really doesn't know what makes America work. Their policies are failing here and everywhere in the world they've been tried. Their solution? Keep trying and keep failing.

Make no mistake: the other side will fight with all their strength to win, to keep power and control in Washington, D.C., and they will vilify anyone who disagrees with them. Their strategy is to demonize citizen activism and to tag the Tea Party and other conservative activist groups as racist, radical, violent, rich, obstructionist—to essentially create different right-wing boogeymen they can hang around the neck of every Republican. Americans who disagree with the Democrats' agenda must be painted as fanatical Tea Party operatives. Bankrupt in their collectivist ideology, such smearing and dirty tactics are really the only thing the other side has left, and their attacks will no doubt become worse.

For example, our opponents have already demonstrated that they will not hesitate to resort to threats, including acts of violence and vandalism. When introducing President Obama to union workers on Labor Day 2011, Teamsters president Jim Hoffa almost braggingly indicated he was ready to use union thuggery to get his way. The *Wall Street Journal* reported:

> Rousing the crowd Mr. Hoffa said that workers' rights are being eroded by Republicans allied with the tea party movement, and urged the union crowd to vote them out of office. But the language turned militaristic.
>
> "We've got to keep an eye on the battle that we face—a war on workers," he said. "You see it everywhere. It is the tea party." And he mentioned that "one thing about working people is, we like a good fight."
>
> To Mr. Obama, Mr. Hoffa said: "President Obama, this is your army, and we are ready to march."
>
> Addressing workers, he went on: "Everybody here's got a vote. If we go back, and we keep the eye on the prize, let's take these son-of-a-bitches out and give America back to America where we belong."[2]

Freedom-loving Americans must always renounce violence of any kind. When we say *fight*, we mean that we should stand up for what we know is right. We do battle with our ideas, our voices, and our votes. We will draw a clear contrast with our opponents not only by standing for America's first principles and for policies that reflect those principles, but by displaying good character and behavior. God gave us our dignity and individual rights, and we can honor that heritage by demonstrating civility and respect—even to those who don't return that courtesy.

We must be better men and women. We cannot allow ourselves

to become part of the lawlessness, violence, and vandalism we now see so often around the world. There has been a global deterioration of law and order, and we've seen cities in other countries that look like war zones with populations increasingly out of control. Whether in Europe's cradle-to-grave nanny states or in Middle Eastern dictatorships, big government has wrecked economies and sparked rebellion among various peoples around the globe: some wanting more government benefits and others wanting to be free from big government.

Profligate spending and debt have brought several European countries to the brink of bankruptcy and are threatening the survival of the European Union. Yet government workers, and those who are dependent on government entitlements, protest any attempts to reduce their handouts from the state. They have been conditioned by decades of government dependence to expect something for nothing, and as the money runs out, they appear to have little concern for the survival of their nations.

Mark Steyn, a Canadian who seems to understand American exceptionalism better than many Americans, explains what is happening in Europe and now threatens America:

> Nothing makes a citizen more selfish than socially equitable communitarianism: once a fellow's enjoying the fruits of government health care and all the rest, he couldn't give a hoot about the general societal interest; he's got his, and if it's going to bankrupt the state a generation hence, well, as long as they can keep the checks coming till he's dead, it's fine by him. "Social democracy" is, it turns out, explicitly anti-social.[3]

Has America reached a low point from which we cannot escape? Absolutely not! A bankrupt and declining nation is not our inevitable fate. It will happen only if we choose to ignore the threats and refuse to solve our problems. It is time for us to confront the threats and solve the problems. We are Americans and we can create a destiny of freedom and prosperity for generations to come—but only if we make the right choices now.

We must choose to be individuals with character, courage, and competence. We must choose to fight for the principles that have always made America unique and exceptional. And we must choose to elect representatives who will take this fight to Washington.

The world is now questioning if Americans still have what it takes to stand up and reestablish ourselves as Reagan's vision of a "shining city on the hill"—the world's best example of how free people and free markets can build a free and prosperous nation. Are Americans still fit for liberty? Russell Kirk, the great conservative philosopher, explains that not everyone is prepared to live in freedom:

> Liberty forced on a people unfit for it is a curse, bringing anarchy. Not all people are equally entitled to liberty, which is "the noblest and highest reward for the development of our faculties, moral and intellectual."[4]

Historically, America has always been fit for liberty because we've been defined by liberty. We might have many problems, but we can solve them all. We are Americans! However, these problems will not be solved by the same people who created them. Americans who are making this country work—those who are raising families, working hard, paying taxes, volunteering in their communities, and continuously developing their character and skills—it is these Americans who must take back their government before their government takes down their country.

The majority of Americans still understand and believe in the principles of freedom. The only pertinent question is this: will they get active in the political process?

We can win this fight, but only if those who love and understand America are willing to fight. It *is* up to you. It is up to all of us.

It really is now or never.

# Notes

## Introduction. A Call to Action

1. Liberty-tree.ca, http://quotes.liberty-tree.ca/quote_blog/Benjamin .Franklin.Quote.21EA.
2. Liberty-tree.ca, http://quotes.liberty-tree.ca/quotes_about/founder.
3. "2010 General Election Turnout Rates," United States Election Project, George Mason University, January 28, 2011, http:// elections.gmu.edu/Turnout_2010G.html.
4. "Iraq Election Turnout 62%, Officials Say," BBC Mobile News, March 9, 2010, http://news.bbc.co.uk/2/hi/8556065.stm.
5. Jessica Ravitz, "Out-of-wedlock births hit record high," CNN.com, April 8, 2009, http://articles.cnn.com/2009-04-08/living/out .of.wedlock.births_1_out-of-wedlock-unwed-mothers-wedding-dress?_s=PM:LIVING[0].
6. "Why Some Tax Units Pay No Income Tax," Rachel M. Johnson, Jim Nunns, Jeff Rohaly, Eric Toder, Roberton William, Tax Policy Center, July 27, 2011. http://www.taxpolicycenter.org/publica tions/url.cfm?ID=1001547[0].

## 1. America in Peril

1. Brian Blase, "Solving the National Medicaid Crisis," Heritage Foundation, May 6, 2011, http://www.heritage.org/research/ reports/2011/05/solving-the-national-medicaid-crisis.

2. Ibid.

3. Ibid.

4. Biz570.com, "Competitive Enterprise Institute Releases Annual Look at Government Regs," April 18, 2011, http://biz570.com/economy/competitive-enterprise-institute-releases-annual-look-at-government-regs-1.1134086.

5. GW regulatory paper, "Federal Regulatory Spending Continues to Increase," http://wc.wustl.edu/files/wc/RegReport2012Press Release_0.pdf.

6. "True Money Supply, Ludwig von Mises Institute," http://mises .org/content/nofed/chart.aspx.

7. John Melloy, "Adjusted for Inflation, Dollar Hits Fiat-Era Low," Fast Money, CNBC.com, April 28, 2011, http://www.cnbc.com/id/42809381/Adjusted_For_Inflation_Dollar_Hits_Fiat_Era_Low.

8. Barry Eichengreen, "Why the Dollar's Reign Is Near an End," Foreign Exchange Report, *Wall Street Journal*, March 2, 2011, http://online.wsj.com/article/SB10001424052748703313304576132170181 013248.html?mod=WSJ_hp_mostpop_read.

9. Ben Rooney, "IMF Calls for Dollar Alternative," CNNMoney, February 10, 2011, http://money.cnn.com/2011/02/10/markets/dollar/index.htm.

10. "Our View on Kids: When Unwed Births Hit 41%, It's Just Not Right," *USA Today*, January 25, 2011, http://www.usatoday.com/news/opinion/editorials/2011-01-25-editorial25_ST_N.htm.

11. C. E. Rouse, "Labor Market Consequences of an Inadequate Education" (paper, Social Costs of Inadequate Education symposium, Teachers College, Columbia University, New York, NY, October 2005).

12. Robert Rector, "Marriage: America's Greatest Weapon against Child Poverty," Heritage Foundation, September 16, 2010, http://www.heritage.org/research/reports/2010/09/marriage-america-s-greatest-weapon-against-child-poverty.

13. National Institute on Drug Abuse, "NIDA InfoFacts: Understanding Drug Abuse and Addiction," http://www.drugabuse.gov/infofacts/understand.html.

14. Robert Rector, "Welfare Spending Under Boehner Plan," Heritage Foundation, July 20, 2011, http://blog.heritage.org/2011/07/27/welfare-spending-under-the-boehner-plan/.
15. Huma Kahn, "Congress Mulls Cuts to Food Stamps Program Amid Record Number of Recipients," *The Note*, ABC News, May 31, 2011, http://blogs.abcnews.com/thenote/2011/05/congress-mulls-cuts-to-food-stamps-program-amid-record-number-of-recipients.html.

## 2. Remembering Why America Is Exceptional

1. Alexis de Tocqueville, *Tocqueville: Democracy in America*, trans. Arthur Goldhammer (New York: Library of America, 2004).
2. Adam Smith, *The Wealth of Nations* (London: Penquin Books, 1986), 443.
3. Jim DeMint, *Saving Freedom* (Nashville: B&H Publishing Group, 2009), 222.
4. Friedrich A. von Hayek, *The Road to Serfdom* (Chicago: University of Chicago Press, 1944), 29.
5. Ibid., 17–18.
6. Ibid., 20–21.
7. Ibid., 16.
8. DeMint, *Saving Freedom*, 141.
9. Rodney Stark, *The Victory of Reason, How Christianity Led to Freedom, Capitalism and Western Success* (New York: Random House, 2005), 18.
10. Ibid.
11. DeMint, *Saving Freedom*, 142.
12. Ibid.
13. Timothy Keesee and Mark Sidwell, *United States History for Christian Schools* (Greenville, SC: Bob Jones University Press, 1991), 110.
14. De Tocqueville, *Democracy in America* (ed. Heffner), 70.
15. Andrew J. Bacevich, *The Limits of Power: The End of American Exceptionalism* (New York: Metropolitan Books, Henry Holt, 2009), 24–25.

## 3. The Philosophies and Policies That Changed America

1. DeMint, *Saving Freedom*, 43.
2. Milton Friedman Quotes page, Quotation Collection, http://www
   .quotationcollection.com/author/Milton_Friedman/quotes.
3. *Milestone Documents in the National Archives* (Washington, DC:
   National Archives and Records Administration, 1995), 69–73,
   http://www.ourdocuments.gov/doc.php?flash=true&doc=57.
4. Ibid.
5. Ibid.
6. DeMint, *Saving Freedom*, 33.
7. Bacevich, *Limits of Power*, 67.

## 5. Cut Wasteful Spending and Regulatory Red Tape

1. James Gattuso and Diane Katz, "Red Tape Rising: A 2011 Mid-Year
   Report," Heritage Foundation, July 25, 2011, http://www.heritage
   .org/research/reports/2011/07/red-tape-rising-a-2011-mid-year-
   report.
2. Thomas Sowell, "Spilled Milk," National Review Online, February
   1, 2011, http://www.nationalreview.com/articles/258491/spilled-
   milk-thomas-sowell.
3. Mark Johanson, "Lemonade Stands Shut Down Across America:
   What Went Sour?" *International Business Times*, August 2, 2011,
   http://www.ibtimes.com/articles/191020/20110802/lemonade-
   stand-shut-down-illegal-fine-ideas-us-open-appleton-midway
   .htm.

## 6. Freedom Solutions That Work

1. U.S. Department of Education, "10 Facts about K–12 Education
   Funding" (June 2005), http://www2.ed.gov/about/overview/fed/
   10facts/10facts.pdf.
2. National Center for Education Statistics, U.S. Department of Education, "Trends in High School Dropout and Completion Rates

in the United States: 1972–2008" (December 2010), http://nces
.ed.gov/pubsearch/pubsinfo.asp?pubid=2011012.

3. Extrapolated from data provided in Bureau of Labor Statistics,
"Usual Weekly Earnings Summary," July 19, 2011, http://www
.bls.gov/news.release/wkyeng.nr0.htm.

4. Federal Reserve, "2007 Survey of Consumer Finances," available at
http://www.federalreserve.gov/econresdata/scf/scf_2007survey
.htm, table 6.

## 7. The Right Message to America

1. David McCullough, *John Adams* (New York: Simon & Schuster),
358.

## 10. It's Now or Never: Final Challenge

1. Matthew Spalding, *The Founders Almanac* (Washington, D.C.:
Heritage Foundation, 2002), 52.

2. Mary Lu Carnevale, "Hoffa: Fired Up, Ready to…Vote?" Washington Wire, *Wall Street Journal*, September 5, 2011, http://blogs
.wsj.com/washwire/2011/09/05/hoffa-fired-up-ready-to-vote/.

3. Mark Steyn, *America Alone, the End of the World as We Know It*
(Washington, D.C.: Regnery Publishing, 2006), 44.

4. Russell Kirk, *The Conservative Mind, from Burke to Eliot* (Washington, D.C.: Regnery Publishing, 1985), 178.

# For Additional Study

**A Selection of Books Recommended by the Heritage Foundation, the Leadership Institute, and *National Review***

*The Seven Fat Years*, by Robert Bartley
*The Gulag Archipelago*, by Aleksandr I. Solzhenitsyn
*The Law*, by Frederic Bastiat
*Up from Liberalism*, by William F. Buckley, Jr.
*The Closing of the American Mind*, by Allan Bloom
*Suicide of the West*, by James Burnham
*Witness*, by Whittaker Chambers
*Advise and Consent*, by Allen Drury
*Capitalism and Freedom*, by Milton Friedman
*Conscience of a Conservative*, by Barry Goldwater
*The Road to Serfdom*, by F. A. Hayek
*The Fatal Conceit*, by F. A. Hayek
*Economics in One Lesson*, by Henry Hazlitt
*The Conservative Mind*, by Dr. Russell Kirk
*Liberty and Tyranny*, by Mark Levin
*Mere Christianity*, by C.S. Lewis
*Atlas Shrugged*, by Ayn Rand
*The Quest for Community*, by Robert Nisbet
*Knowledge and Decisions*, by Thomas Sowell.

## Understanding the Constitution

The United States Constitution
*Common Sense,* by Thomas Paine
The Federalist Papers, by Alexander Hamilton, James Madison, and
    John Jay
*How to Read the Federalist Papers,* by Anthony Peacock
*The Heritage Guide to the Constitution,* by Edwin Meese

## On Senator DeMint's Bookshelf

*Breach of Trust: How Washington Turns Outsiders into Insiders,*
    by Senator Tom Coburn
*The Freedom Agenda: Why a Balanced Budget Amendment Is Necessary to
    Restore Constitutional Government,* by Senator Mike Lee
*The Tea Party Goes to Washington,* by Senator Rand Paul
*End the Fed,* by Representative Ron Paul
*The Road to Prosperity: How to Grow Our Economy and Revive the
    American Dream,* by Senator Pat Toomey

## More Books by Senator DeMint

*Saving Freedom: We Can Stop America's Slide into Socialism*
*The Great American Awakening: Two Years That Changed America,
    Washington and Me*
*Why We Whisper* (with J. David Woodard)

## Books Cited in *Now or Never*

*The Limits of Power,* by Andrew J. Bacevich
*The American Cause,* by Dr. Russell Kirk
*The Wealth of Nations,* by Adam Smith
*Democracy in America,* by Alexis De Tocqueville
*Liberty Defined,* by Representative Ron Paul
*Meltdown,* by Thomas E. Woods, Jr.

## Recommended Magazines and Newspapers

*The American Spectator*
*The American Conservative*
*The Economist*
*Forbes Magazine*
*Human Events*
*Investor's Business Daily*
*National Review*
*Wall Street Journal*
*Washington Times*
*Washington Examiner*

## Recommended Websites and Blogs

TheAmericanConservative.com
TheBlaze.com
BigGovernment.com
Cato.org
CNSnews.com
DailyCaller.com
Heritage.org
HotAir.com
NationaReview.com
Newsbusters.org
Newsmax.com
PowerLineBlog.com
RealClearPolitics.com
Redstate.com
Spectator.org (American Spectator)
TheRightScoop.com
Townhall.com
WeeklyStandard.com

# About the Contributors

**Pat Toomey** is the junior United States senator from Pennsylvania; he served as representative for Pennsylvania's 15th congressional district from 1999 to 2005 and is the former president of Club for Growth. Toomey's challenge to incumbent Republican senator Arlen Specter in 2010 caused Specter to switch to the Democratic Party due to unfavorable polling numbers, but Specter still lost the general election to Toomey. Toomey is the author of *The Road to Prosperity: How to Grow Our Economy and Revive the American Dream.*

**Marco Rubio** is the junior United States senator from Florida and the former speaker of the Florida House of Representatives. When Rubio challenged Florida governor Charlie Crist in the 2010 Senate race, Crist left the Republican Party and pursued an independent run, yet he still lost the general election to Rubio.

**Mike Lee** is the junior United States senator from Utah and that body's current youngest member. Lee challenged and defeated incumbent Republican senator Bob Bennett in the 2010 GOP primary and went on to win the general election. Lee is the author of *The Freedom Agenda: Why a Balanced Budget Amendment Is Necessary to Restore Constitutional Government.*

# ABOUT THE CONTRIBUTORS

**Rand Paul** is the junior United States senator from Kentucky, an ophthalmologist and the son of Texas congressman Ron Paul. Paul challenged and defeated an establishment-favored candidate in the 2010 Republican primary and won the general election through popular grass-roots support. Paul is the author of *The Tea Party Goes to Washington*.

**Tom Coburn** is the junior United States senator from Oklahoma; he served as representative for Oklahoma's 2nd district from 1995 to 2001. Part of the "Republican Revolution" of 1994, Coburn is an optical doctor and a Southern Baptist deacon. He is the author of *Breach of Trust: How Washington Turns Outsiders into Insiders*.

**Dick Armey**, the representative for Texas's 26th congressional district from 1985 to 2003, served as House majority leader from 1995 to 2003; he was part of the "Republican Revolution" of 1994, co-author of the Contract with America, and is the current chairman of FreedomWorks. Armey is the author of *Price Theory: A Policy-Welfare Approach*, *The Freedom Revolution*, *The Flat Tax*, and *Armey's Axioms;* and co-author of *Give Us Liberty: A Tea Party Manifesto*.

**Frank Luntz** is a political consultant and pollster for Fox News. Luntz's specialty has been described as "testing language and finding words that will help his clients sell their product or turn public opinion on an issue or a candidate," and he is widely regarded as an expert on polling data and political messaging. Luntz is the author of *Words That Work: It's Not What You Say, It's What People Hear*.

**David Zupan** is a grass-roots activist and Tea Party leader from Ohio; he works with the North Shore Patriots, West Shore Tea Party, and Lorain County Tea Party.

**Steve King** has served as representative for Iowa's 5th congressional district since 2003. King has long been an outspoken advocate for conservative causes.

**Jack Hunter** is a columnist for *The American Conservative*, regular contributor to *The Daily Caller*, radio personality for WTMA 1250 AM in Charleston, South Carolina, a frequent guest on Fox Business's *Freedom Watch* with Judge Andrew Napolitano, regular guest on Michael Savage's nationally syndicated radio program *The Savage Nation*, and frequent guest host on the Mike Church Show on Sirius/XM. He assisted Senator Rand Paul with his book *The Tea Party Goes to Washington*.